Lives of Eminent Men

Lives of Eminent Men

John Aubrey

ET REMOTISSIMA PROPE

Hesperus Classics

Hesperus Classics
Published by Hesperus Press Limited
4 Rickett Street, London sw6 1ru
www.hesperuspress.com

Clark's edition, on which this collection is based, first published in 1898
This selection first published by Hesperus Press Limited, 2007

Foreword © Ruth Scurr, 2007

Designed and typeset by Fraser Muggeridge studio
Printed in Jordan by Jordan National Press

isbn: 1-84391-161-2
isbn13: 978-1-84391-161-6

CONTENTS

FOREWORD

If you love English books, you will come, sooner or later, to *Brief Lives*: the vivid, sometimes scurrilous, collection of short biographies that John Aubrey wrote in the last decades of his long life, but failed to publish before his death in 1697. They are mostly male seventeenth-century lives: eminent writers, philosophers, mathematicians, scientists, doctors, astrologers, soldiers, sailors, lawyers, dignitaries of the State and Church of England. There are a few female lives too: named women, commanding their own biography, married to or fathered by famous men, staggeringly beautiful, or 'wondrous wanton'. And there are many more unnamed women, caught between the lines – mothers, sisters, wives, mistresses, daughters, whores.

Ever since the first printed extracts from John Aubrey's *Brief Lives* appeared, as late as 1797, generations of scholars have made wide and grateful use of his colourful anecdotes to bring their seventeenth-century subjects fleetingly to life. The words 'Aubrey says' resound down the centuries to the present day, where they still appear reliably in the introduction or footnotes to new books on Hobbes, Milton, Shakespeare and other luminaries whom he captured for posterity. Generous almost to a fault toward his wide circle of scholarly friends, Aubrey was an unusually modest and self-effacing person. He saw himself as a whetstone for other people's talents, doubted the power of his own mind, doubted even the quality of his distinctive prose, and claimed gratitude to others as his own greatest virtue.

In one respect, however, he was completely confident of making an important and original historical contribution – he knew he was inventing the modern genre of biography.

He cursed the classical tradition of high-style panegyrics and selective eulogies: 'Pox take your orators and poets, they spoile lives & histories.' A Life, he insisted, is a small history in which detail and minutiae are all. Contemporaries criticised him for being 'too minute' or trivial, but Aubrey was convinced that 'a hundred yeare hence that minutenesse will be gratefull'. He was right.

Aubrey was subtle; his prose florid, but precise. Often there are notes to himself to check for further information. Of Desiderius Erasmus, for example, he writes: 'He had the parsonage (ask the value) of Aldington in Kent.' And similarly: 'Mr Andrew Marvell: his father was minister of, I think, Hull (ask).' When he related an anecdote, salacious or otherwise, he was careful to indicate its source, to be sceptical if necessary, and never to stray beyond the story into general inferences about the person concerned. He remained strictly within the frame of the story, anecdote or incident he found revealing, not attempting to interpret definitively, still less judge or account for the Lives he wrote. He set out more modestly to record some true things about each of his subjects and saw himself more as a collector than a writer. 'Now what shall I say, or doe with these pretty collections?', he asked his friend, the Antiquarian Anthony à Wood, as old age encroached.

Aubrey was frightened his unpublished manuscripts would be dissipated and lost after his death, so he thought to put them in the new Ashmolean Museum in Oxford, alongside Elias Ashmole's cabinet of curiosities and rarities. Like all collectors, Aubrey expressed personal taste and sensibility in what he chose to include and exclude from his Lives. But beyond this, he did not impose himself strongly on his subjects. This is one of the reasons it has proved so hard to turn the tables and write about the man who was the first great

English biographer. Another reason is the considerable (wholly characteristic) chaos in which he left his manuscripts. Contemporary scholars are still labouring painstakingly toward definitive editions of Aubrey's works. This selection of his literary lives has been drawn from Andrew Clark's late nineteenth-century edition of *Brief Lives*. Aubrey wanted to get at the truth: 'the naked and plaine trueth, which is here exposed so bare that the very pudenda are not covered, and affords many passages that would raise a blush in a young virgin's cheeke'. Clark was certainly more prudish, remarking: 'The conversation of the people among whom Aubrey moved, although they were gentry both in position and in education, was often vulgar, and occasionally foul, as judged by us.' But perhaps not as judged by us?

Aubrey's autobiography is no less fragmentary, no less vivid, than his other lives. Magic and astrology interested him always and Aubrey went so far as to ascribe the disappointments of his own chaotic life – failure to complete or publish almost all his work, a ruinously broken engagement to an unusually litigious woman, bankruptcy, and the final distressing rupture with his friend and collaborator Anthony à Wood – to the unfortunate astrological aspects under which he was born 'very weak and like to die' in Wiltshire on 12th March 1626: 'His life is more remarkable in an astrological respect than for any advancement of learning, having from his birth (till of late years) been labouring under a crowd of ill directions.'

Aubrey was an intrinsically reactive figure, buffeted often by people with stronger purposes than his own, unable to order his life or work, relatively hopeless at self-advancement, but all the time intensely caught up in responding to the world around him. Generally very sensitive, he was always particularly visually responsive: 'If ever I had been good for anything, 'twould have been a painter, I could fancy a thing so strongly and had so clear an idea of it.' As it turned out, his real genius was for writing, not painting, yet it is the visual aspect of Aubrey's sensibility that explains much of the power of his prose. In his time, he saw people, places, buildings, animals, birds, trees, everything, so vividly, that reading him hundreds of years later, we see it all too.

His life of Hobbes was Aubrey's longest. They first met in Malmesbury when Aubrey was still at school, and their friendship continued until Hobbes's death in 1679. The personal warmth and long acquaintance that lie behind 'this little history of our Malmesbury philosopher' are obvious. The detail that the philosopher Hobbes, when young, had such black hair his schoolmates called him Crow, is irrelevant to the theory of the State, but delightful to know. Even when Aubrey did not know his subjects well (if at all) the details that drew him tended to be intimate. Who would not want to know more of Sir John Denham after learning: 'His eye was a kind of light goose-grey, not big; but it had a strange piercingness, not as to shining and glory, but (like a Momus) when he conversed with you he looked into your very thoughts.' How striking to read of Milton: 'His harmonical and ingenious soul did lodge in a beautiful and well proportioned body.' And of Sir Philip Sidney (whom Aubrey's great uncle remembered): 'He was not only of an excellent wit, but extremely beautiful; he much resembled his sister, but his hair was not red, but a little inclining, viz. a dark amber colour.'

Katherine Philips is a rare woman included among the literary lives in her own right. She had read the Bible before she was four years old and was dead at thirty-three. Aubrey notes her cousin's memory of Katherine: 'Very good natured, not at all high-minded; pretty fat, not tall, reddish face.' The description is distorted a little by family jealousy perhaps, but Aubrey does not comment. He does not need to; it is arresting enough to set it down. Aubrey specialised in such rich details; he knew they would be lost if he did not collect them, and he wanted posterity to be grateful.

– Ruth Scurr, 2007

Lives of Eminent Men

JOHN AUBREY
1626–97

His life is more remarkable in an astrological respect than for any advancement of learning, having from his birth (till of late years) been labouring under a crowd of ill directions: for his escapes of many dangers, in journeys both by land and water, forty years.

He was born (long-lived, healthy kindred) at Easton Piers, a hamlet in the parish of Kington Saint Michael in the hundred of Malmesbury in the county of Wiltshire, his mother's (daughter and heir of Mr Isaac Lyte) inheritance, 12th March (St Gregory's Day), AD 1625, about sun-rising, being very weak and like to die that he was christened before morning prayer.

I got not strength till I was eleven or twelve years old; but had sickness of vomiting, for twelve hours every fortnight for ... years,[1] then about monthly, then quarterly, and at last once in half a year. About twelve it ceased.

When a boy, bred at Easton, an eremitical solitude. Was very curious; his greatest delight to be continually with the artificers that came there (e.g. joiners, carpenters, coopers, masons), and understood their trades.

1634, was entered in his Latin grammar by Mr Robert Latimer, rector of Leigh de la Mere, a mile's fine walk, who had an easy way of teaching: and every time we asked leave to *go forth*, we had a Latin word from him which at our return we were to tell him again – which in a little while amounted to a good number of words. 'Twas my unhappiness in half a year to lose this good informer by his death, and afterwards was under several dull ignorant rest-in-house teachers till 1638, at which time I was sent to Blandford School in Dorset (William Sutton, BD, who was ill-natured).

Here I recovered my health, and got my Latin and Greek, best of any of my contemporaries. The usher had (by chance) a Cowper's Dictionary, which I had never seen before. I was then in Terence. Perceiving his method, I read all in the book where Terence was, and then Cicero – which was the way by which I got my Latin. 'Twas a wonderful help to my fancy, my reading of Ovid's *Metamorphoses* in English by Sandys,[2] which made me understand the Latin the better. Also, I met accidentally a book of my mother's, Lord Bacon's *Essays*, which first opened my understanding as to morals (for Tully's[3] *Offices* was too crabbed for my young years) and the excellence of the style, or hints and transitions.

I was always enquiring of my grandfather of the old time, the roof-loft, etc., ceremonies, of the priory, etc. At eight, I was a kind of engineer; and I fell then to drawing, beginning first with plain outlines, e.g. in drafts of curtains. Then at nine (crossed herein by father and schoolmaster), to colours, having nobody to instruct me; copied pictures in the parlour in a table book ... like.

At Blandford, in idle hours, I drew and painted Bates's ... (ask its name).

I was wont (I remember) much to lament with myself that I lived not in a city, e.g. Bristol, where I might have access to watchmakers, locksmiths, etc. I did not very much care for grammar. I had apprehension enough, but my memory not tenacious. So that then was a promising morn enough of an inventive and philosophical head. I had a musical head, inventive, wrote blank verse, had a strong and early impulse to antiquity (strong impulse to Saturn). My wit was always working, but not adroit for verse. I was exceeding mild of spirit; mightily susceptible of fascination. My idea was very clear; fancy like a mirror, pure crystal water which the least wind does disorder and unsmooth ... so noise or etc. would.

My uncle Anthony Browne's bay nag threw me dangerously the Monday after Easter, 1639. Just before it I had an impulse of the briar under which I rode, which tickled him, at the gap at the upper end of Berylane. Thanks be to God!

1642, 2nd May, I went to Oxford.

Peace.

Looked through logic and some ethics.

1642, *Religio Medici* printed, which first opened my understanding, which I carried to Easton, with Sir K.D.'s *Observations* on it.

But now Bellona thundered, and as a clear sky is sometimes suddenly overstretched with a dismal cloud and thunder, so was this serene peace by the civil wars through the factions of those times; see Homer's *Odyssey*.

In August following my father sent for me home, for fear.

In February following, with much ado I got my father to let me to beloved Oxford again, then a garrison for the king.

I got Mr Hesketh, Mr Dobson's man, a priest, to draw the ruins of Osney two or three ways before 'twas pulled down. Now the very foundation is digged up.

In April I fell sick of the smallpox at Trinity College; and when I recovered, after Trinity week, my father sent for me into the country again: where I conversed with none but servants and rustics and soldiers quartered, to my great grief (*Odi profanum vulgus et arceo*),[4] for in those days fathers were not acquainted with their children. It was a most sad life to me, then in the prime of my youth, not to have the benefit of an ingenious conversation and scarce any good books – almost a consumption. This sad life I did lead in the country till 1646, at which time I got (with much ado) leave of my father to let me go to the Middle Temple, 6th April 1646; admitted

24th June following, Oxford was surrendered, and then came to London many of the king's party, with whom I grew acquainted (many of them I knew before). I loved not debauches, but their martial conversation was not so fit for the muses.

6th November, I returned to Trinity College in Oxford again to my great joy; much was made of by the fellows; had their learned conversation, looked on books, music. Here and at Middle Temple (on and off) I (for the most part) enjoyed the greatest felicity of my life (ingenious youths, as rosebuds, imbibe the morning dew) till December 1648 (Christmas Eve's eve) I was sent for from Oxford home again to my sick father, who never recovered: where I was engaged to look after his country business and solicit a lawsuit.

In 1652, October, my father died, leaving me debts of one thousand eight hundred pounds. And brothers' portions one thousand pounds.

Quid digni feci, hic process viam?[5] Truly nothing; only umbrages, that is, Osney abbey ruins, etc., antiquities. A whetstone, *exsors ipse secandi*,[6] e.g. my universal character: that which was neglected and quite forgotten and had sunk had I not engaged in the work, to carry on the work – name them.

He began to enter in pocket memorandum books philosophical and antiquarian remarks, in 1654, at Llantrithid.

In 1656 I began my lawsuit on the entail in Brecon, which lasted till ..., and it cost me one thousand two hundred pounds.

In 1657 I was to have married Miss K. Ryves, who died when to be married, two thousand pounds or more, besides counting care of her brother, one thousand pounds per annum.

In … I made my will and settled my estate on trustees, intending to have seen the antiquities of Rome and Italy for … years, and then to have returned and married, but *diis aliter visum est superis*.[7] My mother, to my inexpressible grief and ruin, hindered this design, which was my ruin.

My estate scarcely one hundred pounds plus Brecon.

Then debts and lawsuits, work and profit, borrowing of money and perpetual riding. To my praise, I had wonderful credit in the country for money. In … sold manor of Bushelton in Herefordshire to Dr T. Willis. In … sold the manor of Stratford in the same county to Herbert Croft, Lord Bishop of Hereford.

Then in 1664, 11th June, went into France. October, returned. Then Joan Sumner.

Memorandum – J. Aubrey in the year 1666, waiting then upon Joan Sumner to her brother at Seen in Wiltshire, there made a discovery of chalybeate waters and those more impregnated than any waters yet heard of in England. I sent some bottles to the Royal Society in June 1667, which were tried with galls before a great assembly there. It turns so black that you may write legibly with it, and did there, after so long a carriage, turn as deep as a deep claret. The physicians were wonderfully surprised at it, and spoke to me to recommend it to the doctors of the Bath, and in some vice versa. I wrote several times, but to no purpose, for at last I found that, though they were satisfied with the excellency of the waters and what the London doctors said was true, they did not care to have company go from Bath. So I inserted it last year in Mr Lilly's almanac, and towards the later end of summer there came so much company that the village could not contain them, and they are now preparing for building of houses against the next summer. John Sumner says (whose well is the best) that it will be worth to him two hundred pounds per annum. Dr Nehemiah Grew in his *History of the Repository of the Royal Society* mentions this discovery, as also of the iron ore there no taken notice before – 'tis in part iii, chap. 2, page 331.

Then lawsuit with her. Then sold Easton Piers, and the farm at Broad Chalk. Lost five hundred pounds plus two hundred pounds plus goods plus timber. Absconded as a banished man.

Then *in monte Dei videbitur*[8] I was in as much affliction as a mortal could be, and never quiet till all was gone, and I wholly cast myself on God's providence. Monastery. I wished monasteries had not been put down, that the reformers would have been more moderate as to that point. Nay, the Turks have monasteries. Why should our reformers be so severe? Convenience of religious houses – Sir Christopher Wren – fit there should be receptacles and provision for contemplative men; if of five hundred, but one or two. 'Tis compensated. What a pleasure 'twould have been to have travelled from monastery to monastery. The reformers in the Lutheran countries were more prudent than to destroy them (e.g. in Alsace, etc.); they only altered the religion.

But notwithstanding all these embarrassments I did *pian piano*[9] (as they occurred) take notes of antiquity; and having a quick draft, have drawn landscapes on horseback symbolically, e.g. on my journey to Ireland in July, in 1660.

The Earl of Thanet gave me ease at Heathfield.

I had never quiet, nor anything of happiness till divested of all, 1670, 1671: at what time providence raised me (unexpectedly) good friends – the right honourable Nicholas, Earl of Thanet, with whom I was delitescent[10] at Heathfield in Kent near a year, and then was invited …; Sir Christopher Wren; Mr Ogilby; then Edmund Wild, esq. FRS[11] of Glasely Hall,

Salop, took me into his arms, with whom I most commonly take my diet and sweet rests.

In 1671, having sold all and disappointed as aforesaid of moneys I received, I had so strong an impulse to (in good part) finish my *Description of Wilts*, two volumes in folio, that I could not be quiet till I had done it, and that with danger enough, *tanquam canis e Nilo*,[12] for fear of the crocodiles, i.e. bailiffs. – And indeed all that I have done and that little that I have studied have been just after that fashion, so that had I not lived long my want of leisure would have afforded but a slender harvest of ...

A man's spirit rises and falls with his wealth: makes me lethargic.

My stomach was so tender that I could not drink claret without sugar, nor white wine, but would disgorge. It was not well ordered till 1670.

A strange fate that I have laboured under never in my life to enjoy one entire month or six weeks' rest for contemplation.

My studies (geometry) were on horse back, and in the house of office: (my father discouraged me). My head was always working; never idle, and even travelling (which from 1649 till 1670 was never off my horse's back) did glean some observations, of which I have a collection in folio of two quires of paper plus a dust basket, some whereof are to be valued.

His chief virtue, gratitude.

I was never riotous or prodigal; but (as Sir E. Leech said) sloth and carelessness are equivalent to all other vices.

My fancy lay most to geometric. If ever I had been good for anything, 'twould have been a painter, I could fancy a thing so strongly and had so clear an idea of it.

When a boy, he did ever love to converse with old men, as living histories. He cared not for play, but on play days, he gave himself to drawing and painting. At nine, a portraiter; and soon was ...

Real character, things that lay dead, I caused to revive by engaging six or seven ... *fungar vice cotis*,[13] etc.

Whereas very sickly in youth; thanks be to God, healthy from sixteen.

Friends

Anthony Ettrick, Trinity College; Middle Temple, John Lydall; Francis Potter – one hundred letters; Sir John Hoskyns, baronet; Edmund Wyld, esq. of Glasley Hall, *quem summae gratidinis ergo nomino*;[14] Mr Robert Hooke, Gresham College; Mr Thomas Hobbes, 165–; Anthony Wood, 1665; Sir William Petty, my singular friend; Sir James Long, baronet of Draycot; Mr Charles Seymour, father of the duke of Somerset; Sir John Stawell, Middle Temple; Bishop of Salisbury (Seth Ward); Dr William Holder.

Works

'The Natural History of Wiltshire'; these 'Lives'; 'Idea of education of the noblesse', in Mr Ashmole's hands; *item*, 'Remainders of Gentilism', being observations on Ovid's *Fastorum*; *memorandum, 'Villare Anglicanum* interpreted'; *item, Faber Fortunae* (for his own private use).

J.A. lived most at Broad Chalk; sometimes at Easton Piers; at London every term. Much of his time spent in journeying to South Wales (entail) and Herefordshire. I now indulge my genius with my friends and pray for the young *angels*. Rest at Mrs More's near Gresham College (Mrs More's in Hammond Alley near Bishopsgate Street farthest house opposite to old Jairer tavern).

I expect preferment through Sir Llewellyn Jenkins.

It was J.A. that did put Mr Hobbes upon writing his treatise *De Legibus*,[15] which is bound up with his *Rhetoric* that one cannot find it but by chance; no mention of it in the first title.

I have written '*An Idea of the Education of the Noblesse* from the age of ten (or eleven) till eighteen': left with Elias Ashmole, esquire.

9.15 p.m., Tuesday 5th March 1673, J.A. arrested ... Gardiner, sergeant, a lusty fair-haired solar fellow, proud, insolent, *et omnia id genus*.[16]

25th March, 1675, my nose bled at the left nostril about 4 p.m. I do not remember any event.

31st July, 1677, I sold my books to Mr Littlebury, that is when my imposthume in my head did break.

About fifty, I had imposthume in the head.

Captain Poyntz (for service that I did him to the Earl of Pembroke and the Earl of Abingdon) did very kindly make me a grant of a thousand acres of land in the island of Tobago, 2nd February 1686. He advised me to send over people to plant and to get subscribers to come in for a share of these one thousand acres, for two hundred acres he says would be enough for me. In this delicate island is the mother of silver.

William Penn, Lord Proprietor of Pennsylvania, did, *ex mero moyu et ex gratia speciali*,[17] give me (16—) a grant, under his seal, of six hundred acres in Pennsylvania, without my seeking or dreaming of it. He advised me to plant it with French protestants for seven years gratis and afterwards they are to pay such a rent. Also he tells me, for two hundred acres ten pounds per annum rent for ever, after three years.

John Aubrey, 20th March, 1693, about eleven at night robbed and fifteen wounds in my head.

5th January, 1694, an apoplectic fit, around 4 p.m.

Born at Easton Piers, 12th March, 1626, about sun-rising: very weak and like to die, and therefore christened that morning before prayer. I think I have heard my mother say I had an ague shortly after I was born.

1629: About three or four years old, I had a grievous ague. I can remember it. I got not health till eleven or twelve: but had sickness and vomiting for twelve hours every fortnight for … years; then, it came monthly for … years; then quarterly; and then, half-yearly; the last was in June 1642. This sickness nipped my strength in the bud.

1633: Eight years old, I had an issue (natural) in the coronal suture of my head, which continued running till twenty-one.

1634: October: I had a violent fever that was like to have carried me off. 'Twas the most dangerous sickness that I ever had.

About 1639 (or 1640) I had the measles, but that was nothing: I was hardly sick.

1639: Monday after Easter week my uncle's nag ran away with me, and gave a very dangerous fall.

1642: 3rd May entered at Trinity College, Oxford.

1643: April and May, the smallpox at Oxford; and shortly after, left that ingenious place; and for three years led a sad life in the country.

1646: April …, admitted to the Middle Temple. But my father's sickness, and business, never permitted me to make any settlement to my study.

1651: About the 16th or 18th of April, I saw that incomparable good-conditioned gentlewoman, Miss M. Wiseman, with whom at first sight I was in love – *haeret lateri*.[18]

1652: 21st October: my father died.

1655: (I think) 14th June, I had a fall at Epsom, and broke one of my ribs and was afraid it might cause an aposthumation.

1656: September 1655, or rather (I think) 1656, I began my chargeable and tedious lawsuit about the entail in Brecknockshire and Monmouthshire.

This year, and the last, was a strange year to me, and of contradictions; that is love M.W. and lawsuits.

1656: December: the disease of love.

1657: 27th November, Katherine Ryves died, with whom I was to marry; to my great loss.

1659: March or April, like to break my neck in Ely minster, and the next day, riding a gallop there, my horse tumbled over and over, and yet (I thank God) no hurt.

1660: July, August, I accompanied A. Ettrick into Ireland for a month; and returning were like to be shipwrecked at Holyhead, but no hurt done.

1661, 1662, 1663: about these years I sold my estate in Herefordshire.

…: January, had the honour to be elected Fellow of the Royal Society.

1664: June 11th, landed at Calais. In August following, I had a terrible fit of the spleen, and piles, at Orleans. I returned in October.

1664, or 1665: Monday after Christmas was in danger to be spoiled by my horse, and the same day received a wound in the testicles which was like to have been fatal. Ask R. Wiseman when – I believe 1664.

1665: 1st November; I made my first address (in an ill hour) to Joan Sumner.

1666: this year all my business and affairs ran kim kam. Nothing took effect, as if I had been under an ill tongue. Treacheries and enmities in abundance against me.

1667: December …: arrested in Chancery Lane, at Mrs Sumner's suite.

1668: 24th February, a.m. about eight or nine, trial with her at Salisbury. Victory at six hundred pounds damage, though devilish opposition against me.

1668: 6th July, was arrested by Peter Gale's malicious contrivance, the day before I was to go to Winchester for my second trial, but it did not retain me above two hours; but did not then go to trial.

1669: 5th March, was my trial at Winchester, from eight to nine, the judge being exceedingly made against me, by my Lady Hungerford. But four of the venue appearing, and with much ado, got the moiety of Salisbury, verdict viz. three hundred pounds.

1669 and 1670: I sold all my estate in Wiltshire.

From 1670, to this very day (I thank God), I have enjoyed a happy delitescency.

1671: danger of arrests.

1677: later end of June, an imposthume broke in my head.

Memorandum – St John's night, 1673, in danger of being run through with a sword by a young gallant at Mr Burges' chamber in the Middle Temple.

Ask the year that I lay at Miss Neve's; for that time I was in great danger of being killed by a drunkard in the street opposite Gray's Inn gate – a gentleman whom I never saw before, but (thanks be to God) one of his companions hindered his thrust. (Memorandum – horoscope thus.)

Danger of being killed by William, Earl of Pembroke, then Lord Herbert, at the election of Sir William Salkeld for New Salisbury.

I see Mars in … threatens danger to me from falls.

I have been twice in danger of drowning.

FRANCIS BACON
LORD ST ALBANS
1561–1626

In his lordship's prosperity Sir Fulke Greville, Lord Brooke, was his great friend and acquaintance; but when he was in disgrace and want, he was so unworthy as to forbid his butler to let him have any more small beer, which he had often sent for, his stomach being nice, and the small beer of Gray's Inn not liking his pallet. This had done his memory more dishonour than Philip Sidney's friendship engraved on his monument has done him honour.

Richard, Earl of Dorset, was a great admirer and friend of the Lord Chancellor Bacon, and was wont to have Sir Thomas Billingsley along with him to remember and to put down in writing my lord's sayings at table.

Mr Ben Jonson was one of his friends and acquaintances, as appears by his excellent verses on his lordship's birthday in his second volume and in his *Underwoods*, where he gives him a character and concludes that 'about his time, and within his view were borne all the wits that could honour a nation or help study.'

He came often to Sir John Danvers at Chelsea. Sir John told me that when his lordship had wrote the *History of Henry VII*, he sent the manuscript copy to him to desire his opinion of it before 'twas printed. Said Sir John 'Your lordship knows that I am no scholar.' "Tis no matter,' said my lord, 'I know what a scholar can say; I would know what *you* can say.' Sir John read it, and gave his opinion what he misliked which Tacitus did not omit (which I am sorry I have forgotten) which my lord acknowledged to be true, and mended it: 'Why,' said he, 'a scholar would never have told me this.'

Mr Thomas Hobbes (of Malmesbury) was beloved by his lordship, who was wont to have him walk with him in his delicate groves where he did meditate: and when a notion darted into his mind, Mr Hobbes was presently to write it down, and his lordship was wont to say that he did it better than anyone else about him; for that many times, when he read their notes he scarce understood it not clearly themselves.

In short, all that were *great and good* loved and honoured him.

Sir Edward Coke, Lord Chief Justice, always envied him, and would be undervaluing his law, as you may find in my lord's letters, and I knew old lawyers that remembered it.

He was Lord Protector during King James's progress into Scotland, and gave audience in great state to ambassadors in the banqueting house at Whitehall.

His lordship would many times have music in the next room where he meditated.

The aviary at York House was built by his lordship; it did cost three hundred pounds.

At every meal, according to the season of the year, he had his table strewed with sweet herbs and flowers, which he said did refresh his spirits and his memory.

When his lordship was at his country house at Gorhambury, St Albans seemed as if the court were there, so nobly did he live. His servants had liveries with his crest (a boar); his watermen were more employed by gentlemen than any other, even the king's.

King James sent a buck to him, and he gave the keeper fifty pounds.

He was wont to say to his servant Hunt, (who was a notable thrifty man, and loved this world, and the only servant he had that he could never get to become bound for him), 'The world was made for man, Hunt; and not man for the world.' Hunt left an estate of one thousand pounds per annum in Somerset.

None of his servants dared appear before him without Spanish leather boots: for he would smell the calf's leather, which offended him.

The East India merchants presented his lordship with a cabinet of jewels, which his page, Mr Cockaine, received, and deceived his lord.

Three of his lordship's servants kept their coaches, and some kept racehorses – see Sir Anthony Welden's *Court of King James*.

He was a homosexual. His Ganymedes and favourites took bribes; but his lordship always gave judgement *secundum aequum et bonum*.[19] His decrees in Chancery stand firm, i.e. there are fewer of his decrees reversed than of any other chancellor.

His dowager married her gentleman usher, Sir (Thomas I think) Underhill, whom she made deaf and blind with too much of Venus. She was living since the beheading of the late king.[20] – Ask where and when she died.

He had a delicate, lively hazel eye; Dr Harvey told me it was like the eye of a viper.

I have now forgotten what Mr Bushell said, whether his lordship enjoyed his Muse best at night, or in the morning.

His lordship was a good poet, but concealed, as appears by his letters. See excellent verses of his lordship's which Mr Farnaby translated into Greek, and printed both in his anthology, that is

The world's a Bubble, and the life of a man
 Less than a span;
In his conception wretched, from the wombe
 So to the tombe;

17

Curst from his cradle, and brought up to yeares,
*   With cares and fears.*
Who then to frail mortality shall trust
But limmes in water or but writes in dust.

Yet since with sorrow here we live opprest,
*   What life is best?*
Courts are but onely superficiall scholes
*   To dandle fooles;*
The rurall parts are turn'd into a den
*   Of savage men;*
And wher's a city from all vice so free,
But may be termed the worst of all the three?

Domestick cares afflict the husband's bed
*   Or pains his hed;*
Those that live single take it for a curse,
*   Or doe things worse;*
Some would have children; those that have them mone,
*   Or wish them gone.*
What is it then to have, or have no wife,
But single thraldome or a double strife?

Our owne affections still at home to please
*   Is a disease;*
To crosse the sea to any foreine soyle,
*   Perills and toyle;*
Warres with their noise affright us; when they cease
*   W'are worse in peace.*
What then remaines? but that we still should cry
Not to be borne, or, being borne, to dye.

At the end of his *Novum Organum* Hugh Holland wrote these verses

Hic liber est qualis potuit non scribere Stultus,
Nec voluit Sapiens : sic cogitavit Hugo.[21]

Sayings

His lordship being in York House garden looking on fishers as they were throwing their net, asked them what they would take for their draught; they answered *so much*: his lordship would offer them no more but *so much*. They drew up their net, and in it were only two or three little fishes: his lordship then told them it had been better for them to have taken his offer. They replied, they hoped to have a better draught; 'but,' said his lordship, 'hope is a good breakfast, but an ill supper.'

When his lordship was in disfavour, his neighbours hearing how much he was indebted, came to him with a motion to buy Oak Wood of him. His lordship told them, 'he would not sell his feathers'.

The Earl of Manchester being removed from his place of Lord Chief Justice of the Common Pleas to be Lord President of the Council, told my lord (upon his fall) that he was sorry to see him made such an example. Lord Bacon replied 'It did not trouble him since *he* was made a *president.*'

The Bishop of London did cut down a noble cloud of trees at Fulham. The Lord Chancellor told him that he was 'a good expounder of dark places'.

Upon his being in disfavour his servants suddenly went away; he compared them to the flying of the vermin when the house was falling.

One told his lordship it was now time to look about him. He replied, 'I do not look *about* me, I look *above* me.'

Sir Julius Caesar (Master of the Rolls) sent to his lordship in his necessity a hundred pounds for a present. His lordship would often drink a good draught of strong beer (March beer) to-bedwards, to lay his working fancy asleep: which otherwise would keep him from sleeping great part of the night.

I remember Sir John Danvers told me, that his lordship much delighted in his curious garden at Chelsea, and as he was walking there one time, he fell down in a dead swoon. My Lady Danvers rubbed his face, temples, etc. and gave him cordial water: as soon as he came to himself, said he, 'Madam, I am no good *footman*.'

His Death and Burial

Mr Hobbs told me that the cause of his lordship's death was trying an experiment: viz., as he was taking the air in a coach with Dr Witherbone (a Scotchman, physician to the king) towards Highgate, snow lay on the ground, and it came into my lord's thoughts, why flesh might not be preserved in snow, as in salt. They were resolved they would try the experiment presently. They alighted out of the coach, and went into a poor woman's house at the bottom of Highgate hill, and bought a hen, and made the woman exenterate it, and then stuffed the body with snow, and my lord did help to do it himself. The snow so chilled him, that he immediately fell so extremely ill, that he could not return to his lodgings (I suppose then at Gray's Inn), but went to the Earl of Arundel's house at Highgate, where they put him into a good bed warmed with a pan, but it was a damp bed that had not been lain in in about a year before, which gave him such a cold that, in two or three days, as I remember he told me, he died of suffocation.

His Residences

I will write something of St Albans, and his house at Gorhambury.

At St Albans is to be seen, in some few places, some remains of the wall of this city; which was in compass about … miles. This magnanimous Lord Chancellor had a great mind to have it made a city again: and he had designed it, to be built with great uniformity: but Fortune denied it to him, though she provided kinder to the great Cardinal Richelieu, who lived both to design and finish that specious town of Richelieu, where he was born; before, an obscure and small village. (The iconography, etc., of this town and palace is nobly engraved.)

Within the bounds of the walls of this old city of St Albans (his lordship's barony) was Verulam House, about half a mile from St Albans; which his lordship built, the most ingeniously contrived little pile, that I ever saw. No question but his lordship was the chiefest architect; but he had for his assistant a favourite of his (a St Albans man) Mr Dobson (who was his lordship's right hand) a very ingenious person (Master of the Alienation Office); but he spending his estate upon women, necessity forced his son William Dobson to be the most excellent painter that England has yet bred.

The view of this house from the entrance into the gate by the highway is thus. The parallel sides answer one another. I do not well remember if on the east side there were bay windows, which his lordship much affected, as may be seen in his essay *Of Building*. Ask whether the number of windows on the east side were five or seven: to my best remembrance but five.

Verulam House

This house did cost nine or ten thousand the building, and was sold about 1665 or 1666 by Sir Harbottle Grimston, baronet, (now Master of the Rolls) to two carpenters for four hundred pounds; of which they made eight hundred pounds. Memorandum – there were good chimney pieces; the rooms very lofty, and all were very well wainscoted. Memorandum – there were two bathing rooms or stuffs, whither his lordship retired afternoons as he saw cause. All the tunnels of the chimneys were carried into the middle of the house, as in this draft; and round about them were seats. The top of the house was well leaded. From the leads[22] was a lovely prospect to the ponds, which were opposite to the east side of the house, and were on the other side of the stately walk of trees that leads to Gorhambury House: and also over that long walk of trees, whose tops afford a most pleasant variegated verdure, resembling the works in Irish stitch. The kitchen, larder, cellars, etc., are underground. In the middle of this house was a delicate staircase of wood, which was curiously carved, and on the post of every interstice was some pretty figure, as of a grave divine with his book and spectacles, a mendicant friar, etc. – (not one thing twice). Memorandum – on the doors of the upper storey on the outside (which were painted dark umber) were the figures of the gods of the Gentiles (viz. on the south door, second storey, was Apollo; on another, Jupiter with his thunderbolt, etc.) bigger than life, and done by an excellent hand; the heightenings were of hatchings of gold, which when the sun shone on them made a most glorious show.

Memorandum – the upper part of the uppermost door, on the east side, had inserted into it a large looking glass, with which the stranger was very gratefully deceived, for (after he had been entertained a pretty while, with the prospects of the ponds, walks and country, which this door faced) when you were about to return into the room, one would have sworn at first glance that he had beheld another prospect through the house: for, as soon as the stranger was landed on the balcony, the concierge that showed the house would shut the door to put this fallacy on him with the looking glass. This was his lordship's summer house: for he says (in his essay) one should have seats for summer and winter as well as clothes.

From hence to Gorhambury is about a little mile, the way easily ascending, hardly so sloping as a desk.

From hence to Gorhambury in a straight line lead three parallel walks: in the middlemost three coaches may pass abreast: in the wing walks two may. They consist of several stately trees of the like growth and height, viz. elm, chestnut, beach, hornbeam, Spanish ash, cervice tree, etc., whose tops (as aforesaid) do afford from the walk on the house the finest show that I have seen, and I saw it about Michaelmas, at which time of the year the colour of leaves are most varied.

The figures of the ponds were thus: they were pitched at the bottoms with pebbles of several colours, which were worked in to several figures, as of fishes, etc. which in his lordship's time were plainly to be seen through the water, now overgrown with flags and rushes.

If a poor body had brought his lordship half a dozen pebbles of a curious colour, he would give them a shilling, so curious was he in perfecting his fish ponds, which I guess do contain four acres. In the middle of the middlemost pond, in the island, is a curious banqueting house of Roman architecture, paved with black and white marble; covered with Cornish slate, and neatly wainscoted.

Memorandum – about the midway from Veralum House to Gorhambury, on the right hand, on the side of the hill which faces the passer by, are set in artificial manner the aforenamed trees, whose diversity of greens on the side of the hill are exceeding pleasant. These delicate walks and prospects entertain the eye to Gorhambury House, which is a large, well-built Gothic house, built (I think) by Sir Nicholas Bacon, Lord Keeper, father to this Lord Chancellor, to whom it descended by the death of Anthony Bacon, his middle brother, who died sans issue. The Lord Chancellor made an addition of a noble portico, which fronts the garden to the south: opposite to every arch of this portico, and as big as the arch, are drawn, by an excellent hand (but the mischief of it is, in watercolours), curious pictures, all emblematical, with mottos under each: for example, one I remember is a ship tossed in a storm, the motto, *Alter erit tum Tiphys*.[23] Enquire for the rest.

Over this portico is a stately gallery, whose glass windows are all painted; and every pane with several figures of beast, bird or flower: perhaps his lordship might use them as topics for local memory. The windows look into the garden, the side opposite to them, no window, but that side is hung all with pictures at length, as of King James, his lordship, and several illustrious persons of his time. At the end you enter is no window, but there is a very large picture, thus: in the middle on a rock in the sea stands King James in armour, with his regal ornaments; on his right hand stands (but whether or no on a rock I have forgotten) King Henry IV of France, in armour; and on his left hand, the King of Spain, in like manner. These figures are (at least) as big as the life, they are done only with umber and shell gold: all the heightening and illumined part being burnished gold, and the shadowed umber, as in the pictures of the gods on the doors of the Verulam House. The roof of this gallery is semi-cylindric, and painted by the same hand and same manner, with heads and busts of Greek and Roman emperors and heroes.

In the hall (which is of the ancient building) is a large story very well painted of the feasts of the gods, where Mars is caught in a net by Vulcan. On the wall, over the chimney, is painted an oak with acorns falling from it; the word, *Nisi quid potius*.[24] And on the wall, over the table, is painted Ceres teaching the sowing of corn; the word *Moniti meliora*.[25]

The garden is large, which was (no doubt) rarely planted and kept in his lordship's time. Here is a handsome door, which opens into Oak Wood. The oaks of this wood are very great and shady. His lordship much delighted himself here: under every tree he planted some fine flower, or flowers, some whereof are there still (1656), viz., peonies, tulips ...

From this wood a door opens into ..., a place as big as an ordinary park, the west part whereof is coppice wood, where are walks cut out as straight as a line and broad enough for a coach, a quarter of a mile long or better. Here his lordship much meditated, his servant Mr Bushell attending him with his pen and ink horn to set down his present notions.

The east of this parquet (which extends to Veralum House) was heretofore, in his lordship's prosperity, a paradise; now it is a large ploughed field. This eastern division consisted of several parts; some thickets of plum trees with delicate walks; some of raspberries. Here was all manner of fruit trees that would grow in England; and a great number of choice forest trees; as the wild ash, sorb, cervice, etc., yew. The walks, both in the coppices and other boscages were most ingeniously designed: at several good views were erected elegant summer houses well built of Roman architecture, well wainscoted and ceiled; yet standing, but defaced, so that one would have thought the barbarians had made a conquest here. This place in his lordship's time was a sanctuary for pheasants, part-ridges, etc., birds of several kinds and countries, as white, speckled, and other partridges. In April, and the springtime, his lordship would, when it rained, take his coach (open) to receive the benefit of irrigation, which he was wont to say was very wholesome because of the nitre in the air and the 'universal spirit of the world'.

His lordship was wont to say, 'I will lay my manor of Gorhambury on't', to which Judge ... made a spiteful reply, saying he would not hold a wager against that, but against *any other* manor of his lordship's he would. Now this illustrious Lord Chancellor had only this manor of Gorhambury.

ROBERT BURTON
1577–1640

Mr Robert Hooke of Gresham College told me that he lay in the chamber in Christ Church that was Mr Burton's, of whom 'tis whispered that not withstanding all his astrology and his book of melancholy, he ended his days in that chamber by hanging himself.

WILLIAM CAMDEN
1551–1623

Mr William Camden, Clarenceux Herald.

Mr Edward Bagshawe (who had been second schoolmaster of Westminster School) has told me that Mr Camden had first his place and his lodgings (which is the gatehouse by the Queen's Scholars' chamber in Dean's Yard), and was after made the head schoolmaster of that school, where he wrote and taught *Institutio Graecae Grammatices Compendiaria: in usum Regiae Scholae Westmonasteriensis*, which is now the common Greek grammar of England, but his name is not set to it. Before, they learned the prolix Greek Grammar of Cleonard.

'Tis reported, that he had bad eyes (I guess lippitude[26]) which was a great inconvenience to an antiquary.

Mr Nicholas Mercator has Stadius' *Ephemerides*, which had been one of Mr Camden's; his name is there (I know his hand) and there are some notes by which I find he was astrologically given.

In his *Britannia* he has a remarkable astrological observation, that when Saturn is in Capricorn a great plague is certainly in London. He had observed it all his time, and sets down the like made by others before his time. Saturn was so posited in the great plague 1625, and also in the last great plague 1665. He likewise delivers that when an eclipse happens in Scorpio, that 'tis fatal to the town of Shrewsbury.

He was basted by a courtier of the queen's in the cloisters at Westminster for denigrating Queen Elizabeth in his history – from Dr John Earle, Dean of Westminster.

My honoured and learned friend, Thomas Fludd, esq., a Kentish gentleman, was neighbour and acquaintance to Sir Robert Filmore, in Kent, who was very intimately acquainted with Mr Camden, who told Sir Robert that he was not suffered to print many things in his *Elisabetha*, which he sent over to his acquaintance and correspondent Thuanas, who printed it faithfully in his *Annals* without altering a word.

Mr Camden much studied the Welsh language and kept a Welsh servant to improve him in that language, for the better understanding of our antiquities. – From Samuel Butler.

Sir William Dugdale tells me that he has minutes of King James's life to a month and a day, written by Mr William Camden; as also his own life, according to years and days, which is very brief, but two sheets, Mr Camden's own handwriting. Sir William Dugdale had it from John Hacket, Bishop of Coventry and Lichfield, who did filch it from Mr Camden as he lay dying.

GEOFFREY CHAUCER
1328–1400

Sir Hamond L'Estrange had his works in MS, a most curious piece, most rarely written and illumined, which he valued at one hundred pounds. His grandson and heir still has it. – From Mr Roger L'Estrange.

He taught his son the use of the astrolabe at ten; see his treatise on the astrolabe.

Dunnington Castle, near Newbury, was his; a noble seat and strong castle, which was held by the king (Charles I) (who was governor?) but since dismantled.

Near this castle was an oak, under which Sir Geoffrey was wont to sit, called 'Chaucer's Oak', which was cut down under Charles I; and so it was, that the culprit was called into the star chamber and was fined for it. Judge Richardson harangued against him long, and like an orator, had topics from the Druids, etc. This information I had from an able attorney that was at the hearing.

One Mr Goresuch of Woodstock dined with us at Romney Marsh, who told me that at the old Gothic-built house near the park gate at Woodstock, which was the house of Sir Geoffrey Chaucer, that there is his picture, which goes with the house from one to another – which see.

JOHN CLEVELAND
1613–58

John Cleveland was born in Warwickshire. He was a fellow at St John's College in Cambridge, where he was more taken notice of for his being an eminent disputant, than a good poet. Being turned out of his fellowship for a malignant[27] he came to Oxford, where the king's army was, and was much caressed by them. He went thence to the garrison at Newark upon Trent, where upon some occasion of drawing of articles, or some writing, he would needs add a short conclusion, viz. 'and hereunto we annex our lives, as a label to our trust'. After the king was beaten out of the field, he came to London, and retired in Gray's Inn. He and Samuel Butler, etc. of Gray's Inn, had a club every night. He was a comely plump man, good curled hair, dark brown. Died of the scurvy, and lies buried in St Andrew's Church in Holborn.

JOHN COLET
1467–1519

After the conflagration, his monument being broken, his coffin, which was lead, was full of a liquor that conserved the body. Mr Wyld and Ralph Greatorex tasted it and 'twas a kind of insipid taste, something of an ironish taste. The body felt, to the probe of a stick that they thrust into a chink, like brawn. The coffin was of lead and laid in the wall about two and a half feet above the surface of the floor.

RICHARD CORBET
1583–1635

Richard Corbet, DD, was the son of Vincent Corbet, who was a gardener at Twickenham, as I have heard my old cousin Whitney say. See in Ben Jonson's *Underwoods* an epitaph on this Vincent Corbet, where he speaks of his nurseries, etc.

He was a Westminster scholar; old parson Bussey, of Alscott in Warwickshire, went to school with him – he would say that he was a very handsome man, but something apt to abuse, and a coward.

He was a student of Christ Church in Oxford. He was very facetious, and a good fellow. One time he and some of his acquaintances being merry at Friar Bacon's study (where was good liquor sold), they were drinking on the leads of the house, and one of the scholars was asleep, and had a pair of good silk stockings on. Dr Corbet (then MA, if not BD) got a pair of scissors and cut them full of little holes, but when they other awoke, and perceived how and by whom he was abused, he did chastise him, and made him pay for them.

After he was Doctor of Divinity, he sang ballads at the cross at Abingdon on a market day. He and some of his comrades were at the tavern by the cross, (which by the way was then the finest of England; I remember it when I was a freshman; it was admirable curious Gothic architecture, and fine figures in the niches: 'twas one of those built by king … for his queen). The ballad singer complained he had no custom, he could not put off his ballads. The jolly doctor puts off his gown, and puts on the ballad singer's leathern jacket, and being a handsome man, and had a rare full voice, he presently sold a great many, and had a great audience.

After the death of Dr William Goodwin, he was made dean of Christ Church (ask if ever canon).

He had a good interest with great men, as you may find in his poems, and with the then great favourite, the Duke of Buckingham; his excellent wit was letters of recommendation to him. I have forgotten the story, but at the same time that Dr Samuel Fell thought to have carried it,[28] Dr Corbet put a pretty trick on him to let him take a journey on purpose to London for it, when he already had grant of it.

He preached a sermon before the king at Woodstock (I suppose King James, query) and no doubt with a very good grace; but it happened that he was out,[29] on which occasion there were made these verses –

A reverend Deane
With his Ruffe starch't cleane,
Did preach before the King;
In his Band-string was spied
A Ring that was tyed,
Was not that a pritty thing?
The Ring without doubt,
Was the thing putt him out,
So oft hee forgot what was next;
For all that were there,
On my conscience dare sweare
That he handled it more than his Text.

His conversation was extremely pleasant. Dr Stubbins was one of his cronies; he was a jolly fat doctor and a very good housekeeper; parson of Ambrosden in Oxfordshire. As Dr Corbet and he were riding in Lob Lane in wet weather ('tis an extraordinarily deep dirty lane) the coach fell; and Dr Corbet said that Dr Stubbins was up to the elbows in mud, he was up to the elbows in Stubbins.

In 1628 he was made Bishop of Oxford, and I have heard that he had an admirable, grave and venerable aspect.

One time, as he was confirming, the country people pressing in to see the ceremony, said he, 'Bear off there, or I'll confirm you with my staff.' Another time, being about to lay his hand on the head of a man very bald, he turns to his chaplain (Lushington) and said, 'Some dust, Lushington,' (to keep his hand from slipping). There was a man with a great venerable beard; said the bishop, 'You, behind the beard.'

His chaplain, Dr Lushington, was a very learned and ingenious man and they loved one another. The bishop sometimes would take the key of the wine cellar, and he and his chaplain would go and lock themselves in and be merry. Then first he lays down his episcopal hat – 'There lies the doctor.' Then he puts of his gown – 'There lies the bishop.' Then 'twas – 'Here's to you, Corbet,' and 'Here's to you, Lushington.' – From Josiah Howe, BD, Trinity College, Oxford.

He built a pretty house near the causeway beyond Friar Bacon's study.

He married Alice Hutton whom 'twas said he begot. She was a very beautiful woman, and so was her mother. He had a son (I think Vincent) that went to school at Westminster, with Ned Bagshawe; a very handsome youth, but he is run out of all, and goes begging up and down to gentlemen.

He was made Bishop of Norwich in 1632. He died 28th July, 1635. The last words he said were, 'Goodnight Lushington.'

His poems are pure natural wit, delightful and easy. It appears by his verses to Master of the Requests Ailesbury, 9th December 1618, that he had knowledge of analytical learning, being so well acquainted with him and the learned Mr Thomas Harriot.

Memorandum – his antagonist Dr Daniel Price, the anniversarist, was made dean of the church at Hereford. Dr William Watts, canon of that church, told me, 1656, that this dean was a mighty pontifical proud man, and that one time when they went in procession about the cathedral church, he would not do it in the usual way in his surplice, hood, etc. on foot, but rode on a mare, thus habited, with the Common Prayer book in his hand, reading. A stone-horse[30] happened to break loose ... he would never ride in procession afterwards.

ABRAHAM COWLEY
1618–67

He was born in Fleet Street, London, near Chancery Lane; his father a grocer.

He was secretary to the Earl of St Albans (then Lord Jermyn) at Paris. When His Majesty returned, the Duke of Buckingham hearing that at Chertsey was a good farm of about ... pounds per annum, belonging to the queen mother, goes to the Earl of St Albans and the commissioners to take lease of it. They answered that 'twas beneath his grace to take a lease of them. That was all one, he would have it, paid for it, and had it, and freely and generously gave it to his dear and ingenious friend, Mr Abraham Cowley, for whom purposely he bought it.

He lies interred at Westminster Abbey, next to Sir Geoffrey Chaucer, where the Duke of Buckingham has put a neat monument of white marble. Above that a very fair urn, with a kind of garland of ivy around it.

By Sir J. Denham –

Had Cowley ne'er spoke nor Tom Killigew writ,
They'd both have made a very good wit.

– A.C. discoursed very ill and with hesitation.

He wrote when a boy at Westminster poems and a comedy called *Love's Riddle*, dedicated to Sir Kenelm Digby.

See his will, that is, for his true and lasting charity, that is, he settles his estate in such a manner that every year so much is to be paid for the enlarging of poor prisoners cast into jail by cruel creditors for some debt. This I had from Mr Dunning of London, a scrivener, who is an acquaintance of Dr Cowley's brother. I do think this memorable benefaction is not mentioned in his life in print before his works; and it is certainly the best method of charity.

SIR WILLIAM DAVENANT
1606–68

Sir William Davenant, knight, Poet Laureate, was born about the end of February in the city of Oxford at the Crown tavern.

His father was John Davenant, a vintner there, a very grave and discreet citizen: his mother was a very beautiful woman, and of very good wit, and of conversation extremely agreeable. They had three sons, Robert, William and Nicholas (an attorney): and two handsome daughters, one married to Gabriel Bridge (BD, fellow of Christ Church College, beneficed in the Vale of the White Horse), another to Dr William Sherburne (minister of Pembridge in Hereford, and a canon of that church).

Mr William Shakespeare was wont to go into Warwickshire once a year, and did commonly in his journey lie at this house in Oxford, where he was exceedingly respected. (I have heard Parson Robert say Mr W. Shakespeare has given him a hundred kisses). Now Sir William would sometimes, when he was pleasant over a glass of wine with his most intimate friends – e.g. Samuel Butler (author of *Hudibras*), etc. – say, that it seemed to him that he wrote with the very spirit that Shakespeare [wrote], and seemed contented enough to be thought his son. (He would tell them the story as above, in which way his mother had a very light report.)

He went to school at Oxford to Mr Sylvester (Charles Whear, son of Diggory Whear, was his schoolfellow), but I fear he was drawn from school before he was ripe enough.

He was preferred to the first Duchess of Richmond to wait on her as a page. I remember he told me, she sent him to a famous apothecary for some Unicorn's horn, which he was resolved to try with a spider that he encircled in it, but without the expected success; the spider would go over, and through and through, unconcerned.

He was next a servant (as I remember, a page also) to Sir Fulke Greville, Lord Brooke, with whom he lived to his death, which was that a servant of his (that had long waited on him and his lordship had often told him that he would do something for him, but did not but still put him off with delays) as he was trussing up his lord's points coming from the lavatory (for then their breeches were fastened to the doublets with points – then came in hooks and eyes – which not to have fastened was in my boyhood a great crime) stabbed him. This was at the same time that the Duke of Buckingham was stabbed by Felton, and the great noise and report of the Duke's, Sir William told me, quite drowned this of his lord's, that it was scarce taken notice of. This Sir Fulke Greville was a good wit, and had been a good poet in his youth. He wrote a poem in folio which he printed not till he was old, and then (as Sir W. said) with too much judgement and refining, spoiled it, which was at first a delicate thing.

He wrote a play or plays, and verses, which he did with so much sweetness and grace, that by it he got the love and friendship of his two Maecenases,[31] Mr Endymion Porter, and Mr Henry Jermyn (since Earl of St Albans), to whom he has dedicated his poem called *Madagascar*. Sir John Suckling also was his great and intimate friend.

After the death of Ben Jonson he was made in his place Poet Laureate.

He got a terrible clap of a black handsome wench that lay in Axe Yard, Westminster, whom he thought on when he speaks of Dalga in *Gondibert*, which cost him his nose, with which unlucky mischance, many wits were too cruelly bold: e.g. Sir John Menis, Sir John Denham etc.

In 1641, when the troubles began, he was fain to fly into France, and at Canterbury he was seized on by the mayor – see Sir John Menis' verses –

For Will had in his face the flawes
And markes received in countrey's cause:
They flew on him like lyons passant
And tore his nose as much as was on't
And called him superstitious groome.
And Popish Dog, and Cur of Rome.
… 'Twas surely the first time
That Will's religion was a crime.

In the civil wars in England he was in the army of William, Marquess of Newcastle (since Duke), where he was general of the ordinance. I have heard his brother Robert say, for that service there was owing to him by King Charles I ten thousand pounds. During that war, 'twas his hap to have two aldermen of York his prisoners, who were something stubborn, and would not give the ransom ordered by the council of war. Sir William used them civilly, and treated them in his tent, and sat them at the upper end of his table *à la mode de France*, and having done so a good while to his charge, told them (privately and friendly) that he was not able to keep so chargeable guests, and bade them take an opportunity to escape, which they did; but having been gone a little way they considered with themselves that in gratitude they ought to go back and give Sir William their thanks; which they did, but it was like to have been to their great danger of being taken by the soldiers; but they happened to get safe to York.

The king's party being overcome, Sir William Davenant (who received the honour of a knighthood from the Duke of Newcastle by commission) went into France; resided chiefly in Paris where the Prince of Wales then was. He then began to write his romance in verse, called *Gondibert*, and had not written above the first book, but being very fond of it, prints it (before a quarter finished), with an epistle of his to Mr Thomas Hobbes and Mr Hobbes' excellent epistle to him before it. The courtiers with the Prince of Wales could never be at quiet about this piece, which was the occasion of a very witty but satirical little book of verses in octavo, about four sheets, written by George, Duke of Buckingham, Sir John Denham, etc.

That thou forsak'st thy sleep, thy diet,
And which is more than that, *our quiet*.

The last word Mr Hobbes told me was the occasion of their writing.

Here he laid an ingenious design to carry a considerable number of artificers (chiefly weavers) from hence to Virginia; and by Mary the queen mother's means, he got favour from the King of France to go into the prisons and choose. So when the poor damned wretches understood what the design was, they cried with one voice: '*tous tisserans!*', i.e. 'we are all weavers!' William took thirty-six, as I remember, if not more and shipped them; and as he was in his voyage towards Virginia, he and his *tisserans* were all taken by the ships then belonging to the Parliament of England. The slaves I suppose they sold, but Sir William was brought prisoner to England. Whether he was first a prisoner at Carisbrooke Castle in the Isle of Wight, or at the Tower of London, I have forgotten: he was prisoner at both. His *Gondibert*, quarto, was finished at Carisbrooke Castle. He expected no mercy from the Parliament, and had no hopes of escaping with his life. It pleased God that the two aldermen of York aforesaid hearing that he was taken and brought to London to be tried for his life, which they understood was in extreme danger, they were touched with so much generosity and goodness, as, upon their own accounts and mere notion, to try what they could to save Sir William's life who had been so civil to them and a means to save theirs, to come to London: and acquainting the Parliament with it, upon their petition, etc., Sir William's life was saved.

Being freed from imprisonment, (because plays, that is tragedies and comedies, were in those Presbyterian times scandalous) he contrives to set up an opera, *stylo recitativo*,[32] wherein Sergeant Maynard and several citizens were backers. It began at Rutland House, in Charterhouse Yard; next (that is in 1656) at the Cockpit in Drury Lane, where were acted very well

38

stylo recitativo, *Sir Francis Drake* and *The Siege of Rhodes* (first and second part). It did affect the eye and ear extremely. This first brought scenes[33] in fashion in England; before, at plays, only a hanging.

In 1660 was the happy restoration of His Majesty Charles II. Then was Sir William made Master of the Revels; and the tennis court in Little Lincoln's Inn field was turned into a playhouse for the Duke of York's players, where Sir William had lodgings, and where he died, 7th April 1668.

I was at his funeral. He had a coffin of walnut tree; Sir John Denham said 'twas the finest coffin that he ever saw. His body was carried in a hearse from the playhouse to Westminster Abbey, where, at the great west door, he was received by the singing men and choristers, who sang the service of the church ('I am the Resurrection', etc.) to his grave, which is in the south cross-aisle, on which, on a paving stone of marble, is written, in imitation of that on Ben Jonson, 'O rare Sir Will. Davenant'.

Sir William has written about twenty-five (ask) plays, the romance called *Gondibert* and a little poem called *Madagascar*.

His private opinion was that religion at last – e.g. a hundred years hence – would come to settlement, and that in a kind of ingenious Quakerism.

Sir William was Poet Laureate; and Mr John Dryden has his place. But I thought it had been proper that a laurel should have been set on his coffin – which was not done.

SIR JOHN DENHAM
1615–69

Sir John Denham, Knight of Bath, was born at Dublin in Ireland, in 1615.

Ask Dr Busby if he was a Westminster scholar – I have forgotten. He was admitted of Trinity College in Oxford. I have heard Mr Josias Howe say that he was the dreamiest young fellow; he never expected such things from him as he has left the world. When he was there he would game extremely; when he had played away all his money he would play away his father's wrought rich gold caps.

His father was Sir John Denham, one of the Barons of the Exchequer. He had been one of the Lords Justices in Ireland: he married Eleanor, one of the daughters of Sir Garret Moore, knight, Lord Baron of Melifont, in the kingdom of Ireland, whom he married during his service in Ireland in the place of Chief Justice there.

From Trinity College he went to Lincoln's Inn, where (as Judge Wadham Windham, who was his contemporary, told me) he was as good a student as any in the house. Was not suspected to be a wit.

At last, viz. 1640, his play of *The Sophy* came out, which did take extremely. Mr Edmund Waller said then of him, he 'broke out like the Irish rebellion – threescore thousand strong', before anybody was aware.

He was much cheated by gamesters, and fell acquainted with that unsanctified crew, to his ruin. His father had some suspicion of it, and chid him severely, whereupon his son John (only child) wrote a little essay in octavo, 'Against gaming and to show the vanities and inconveniences of it', which he presented to his father to let him know his detestation of it. But shortly after his father's death (who left two thousand or one thousand five hundred pounds in ready money, two houses well furnished and much plate), the money was played away first, and next the plate was sold. I remember about 1646 he lost two hundred pounds one night at New Cut. I guess 1642 he was High Sheriff of the county of Surrey.

At the beginning of the civil war he was made governor of Farnham Castle for the king, but he was but a young soldier, and did not keep it. In 1643 after Edgehill fight, his poem called *Cowper's Hill* was printed at Oxford, in a sort of brown paper, for then they could get no better.

1647 (ask) he conveyed, or stole away, the two Dukes of York and Gloucester from St James's (from the tuition of the Earl of Northumberland) and conveyed them into France to the Prince of Wales and the queen mother. King Charles II sent him and the Lord Culpeper envoys to the King of Poland.

In 1652 he returned into England and being in some straits was kindly entertained by the Earl of Pembroke at Wilton, where I had the honour to contract an acquaintance with him. He was, as I remember, a year with my Lord of Pembroke at Wilton and London; he had then sold all the lands his father had left him.

His first wife was the daughter and heir of one Cotton of Gloucestershire, by whom he had five hundred pounds per annum, one son and two daughters.

He was much beloved by King Charles I, who much valued him for his ingenuity. He granted him the reversion of the office of surveyor of His Majesty's buildings, after the decease of Mr Inigo Jones; which place, after the restoration of King Charles II he enjoyed to his death, and got seven thousand pounds, as Sir Christopher Wren told me of, to his own knowledge. Sir Christopher Wren was his deputy.

In 1665 he married his second wife, Margaret Brookes, a very beautiful young lady; Sir John was ancient and limping. The Duke of York fell deeply in love with her, though (I have been morally assured) he never had carnal knowledge of her.

This occasioned Sir John's distemper of madness, which first appeared when he went from London to see the famous freestone quarries at Portland in Dorset, and when he came within a mile of it, turned back to London again, and did not see it. He went to Hounslow, and demanded rents of lands he had sold many years before; went to the king and told him he was the Holy Ghost. But it pleased God that he was cured of this distemper, and wrote excellent verses afterwards. His second lady had no child; was poisoned by the hands of the Countess of Rochester with chocolate.

At the coronation of King Charles II he was made Knight of the Bath.

He died at the house of his office (which he built as also the brick buildings next the street in Scotland Yard), and was buried in 1669, 23rd March, in the south cross-aisle of Westminster Abbey, near Sir Geoffrey Chaucer's monument, but hitherto (1680) without any memorial for him.

Memorandum – the parsonage house at Egham (vulgarly called 'The Place') was built by Baron Denham; a house very convenient, not great, but pretty, and pleasantly situated, and in which his son, Sir John (though he had better seats), did take most delight in. He sold it to John Thynne esq. In this parish is a place called Camomile Hill, from the camomile that grows there naturally; as also west of it is Prunewell Hill (formerly part of Sir John's possessions), where was a fine tuft of trees, a clear spring and a pleasant prospect to the east, over the level of Middlesex and Surrey. Sir John took great delight in this place, and was wont to say (before the troubles) that he would build there a retiring place to entertain his muses; but the wars forced him to sell that as well as the rest. He sold it to Mr Anstey. In this parish, west and by north (above Runnymede) is Cowper's Hill, from whence is a noble prospect, which is incomparably described by that sweet swan, Sir John Denham.

Memorandum – he delighted much in bowls, and did bowl very well.

He was of the tallest, but a little incurvetting at his shoulders, not very robust. His hair was but thin and flaxen, with a moist curl. His gait was slow, and was rather a stalking (he had long legs), which was wont to put me in mind of Horace, *De Arte poetica*:

> *Hic, dum sublimes versus ructatur, et errat*
> *Si veluti merulis intentus decidit auceps*
> *In puteum foveamve:*[34]

His eye was a kind of light goose-grey, not big; but it had a strange piercingness, not as to shining and glory, but (like a Momus) when he conversed with you he looked into your very thoughts.

He was generally temperate as to drinking; but one time when he was a student of Lincoln's Inn, having been merry at the tavern with his comrades, late at night, a frolic came into his head, to get a plasterer's brush and a pot of ink, and blot out all the signs between Temple Bar and Charing Cross, which made a strange confusion the next day, and 'twas in term time. But it happened that they were discovered, and it cost him and them some moneys. This I had from R. Estcott, esq. that carried the inkpot.

In the time of the civil wars, George Withers, the poet, begged Sir John Denham's estate at Egham of the Parliament, in whose cause he was a captain of horse. It happened that G.W. was taken prisoner, and was in danger of his life, having written severely against the king. Sir John Denham went to the king and desired His Majesty not to hang him, for that whilst G.W. lived he should not be the worst poet in England.

Memorandum – in the verses against Gondibert, most of them are Sir John's. He was satirical when he had a mind to it.

RENÉ DESCARTES
1596–1650

How he spent his time in his youth, and by what method he became so knowing, he tells the world in his treatise entitled *Of Method*. The Society of Jesus[35] glory in that their order had the educating of him. He lived several years at Egmont (near The Hague) from whence he dated several of his books. He was too wise a man to encumber himself with a wife; but as he was a man, he had the desires and appetites of a man; he therefore kept a good-conditioned handsome woman that he liked, and by whom he had some children (I think two or three). 'Tis pity, but coming from the brain of such a father, they should be well cultivated. He was so eminently learned that all learned men made visits to him, and many of them would desire him to show them his store of instruments (in those days mathematical learning lay much in the knowledge of instruments, and, as Sir H.S. said, in doing of tricks), he would draw out a little drawer under his table, and show them a pair of compasses with one of the legs broken; and then, for his ruler, he used a sheet of paper folded double. This from Alexander Cowper (brother of Samuel), limner to Christina, Queen of Sweden, who was familiarly acquainted with Descartes.

Mr Hobbes was wont to say that had Descartes kept himself wholly to geometry that he had been the best geometer in the world. He did very much admire him, but said that he could not pardon him for writing in the defence of transubstantiation which he knew to be absolutely against his judgement.

MICHAEL DRAYTON
1563–1631

Michael Drayton esq., born in Warwickshire at Atherton upon Stower (ask Thomas Mariett).

He was a butcher's son. Was a squire; viz. one of the esquires to Sir Walter Aston, Knight of the Bath, to whom he dedicated his poem. Sir J. Brawne was a great patron of his.

He lived at the bay-window house next the east end of St Dunstan's Church in Fleet Street.

Sir Edward Bysshe, Clarenceux Herald, told me he asked Mr Selden once (jestingly) whether he wrote the commentary to his 'Polyolbion' and 'Epistles', or Mr Drayton made those verses to his notes.

See his inscription[36] given by the Countess of Dorset. Mr Marshall, the stonecutter, of Fetter Lane, also told me that these verses were made by Mr Francis Quarles, who was his great friend, and whose head he wrought curiously in plaster, and valued for his sake. 'Tis pity it should be lost. Mr Quarles was a very good man.

SAINT DUNSTAN
925–988

I find in Mr Selden's verses before Hopton's *Concordance of Years*, that he was a Somersetshire gentleman. He was a great chemist.

The story of his pulling the devil by the nose with his tongs as he was in his laboratory was famous in church windows.

He was a Benedictine monk at Glastonbury, where he was afterwards abbot, and after that was made Archbishop of Canterbury. He preached the coronation sermon at Kingston, and crowned King Edwy. In his sermon he prophesied, which the Chronicle mentions.

Mr Meredith Lloyd tells me that there is a book in print of his on the philosopher's stone: ask the name.

Edwardus Generosus gives a good account of him in a manuscript that Mr Ashmole has.

Meredith Lloyd had, about the beginning of the civil war, a MS of this saint's concerning chemistry, and says that there are several MSS of his up and down in England: ask Mr Ashmole.

Edwardus Generosus mentions that he could make a fire out of gold, with which he could set any combustible matter on fire at a great distance. Memorandum – in Westminster library is an old printed book, in folio, of the lives of the old English saints.

Meredith Lloyd tells me that, three or four hundred years ago, chemistry was in a greater perfection much, than now; their process was then more seraphic and universal: now they look only after medicines.

Several churches are dedicated to him: two at London: ask if one at Glastonbury.

DESIDERIUS ERASMUS
1467–1536

His name was 'Gerard Gerard', which he translated into 'Desiderius Erasmus'. He was begot (as they say) behind doors – see an Italian book in octavo, *Of Famous Bastards*. His father (as he says in his life written by himself) was the tenth and youngest of his grandfather, who was therefore designed to be dedicated to God. The father of Gerard lived with Margaret (daughter of a certain Dr Peter) as man and wife (and some would say they were married).

His father took great care to send him to an excellent school, which was at Dusseldorf, in the Duchy of Cleves. He was a tender chit, and his mother would not entrust him at board, but took a house there, and made him cordials, etc. – from John Pell, DD.

He loved not fish, though born in a fish town – from Sir George Ent, MD.

From Dr John Pell – he was of the order of Augustine, whose habit was the same that the pest-house master at Pisa in Italy wore; and walking in that town, people beckoned him to go out of the way, taking him to be the master of the pest-house; and he not understanding the meaning, and keeping on his way, was there by one well basted. He made his complaint when he came to Rome, and had dispensation for his habit.

He studied sometime in Queen's College in Cambridge: his chamber was over the water. Ask Mr Paschal more particularly, and if a fellow: Mr Paschal had his study when a young scholar there.

The stairs that rise up to his study at Queen's College in Cambridge do bring first into two of the fairest chambers in the ancient building; in one of them, which looks into the hall and chief court, the vice-president kept in my time; in that adjoining, it was my fortune to be, when fellow. The chambers over are good lodging rooms; and to one of them is a square turret adjoining, in the upper part of which is that study of Erasmus; and over it leads. To that belongs the best prospect about the college, viz. upon the river, into the cornfields and country adjoining, etc. so that it might very well consist with the civility of the college to that great man (who was no fellow, and I think stayed not long there) to let him have that study. His keeping room might be either the vice-president's, or, to be near to him, the next; the room for his servitor that above, over it; and through it he might go to that study, which for the height and neatness and prospect, might easily take his fancy. This from Mr Andrew Paschal, Rector of Chedzoy in Somerset, 15th June, 1680.

He mentions his being there in one of his *Epistles*, and blames the beer there. One, long since, wrote, in the margin of the book in the college library in which that is said, 'As it was in the beginning,' etc. and all Mr Paschal's times they found fault with the brewer.

He had the parsonage (ask the value) of Aldington in Kent, which is about three degrees perhaps a healthier place than Dr Pell's parsonage in Essex. I wonder they could not find for him better preferment; but I see that the Sun and Aries being in the second house, he was not born to be a rich man.

He built a school in Rotterdam, and endowed it, and ordered the institution. Sir George Ent was educated there. A statue in brass is erected to his memory on the bridge in Rotterdam.

Sir Charles Blount, of Mapledurham, in Oxfordshire (near Reading), was his scholar (in his *Epistles* there are some to him), and desired Erasmus to do him the favour to sit for his picture, and he did so, and it is an excellent piece: which picture my cousin John Danvers, of Baynton (Wiltshire) has. His wife's grandmother was Sir Charles Blount's daughter or granddaughter. 'Twas pity such a rarity should have been aliened from the family, but the issue male is lately extinct. I will sometime or other endeavour to get it for Oxford library.

They were wont to say that Erasmus was suspended between Heaven and Hell, till about the year 1655 (ask Dr Pell), the Conclave at Rome damned him for a heretic, after he had been dead a hundred and twenty years.

His deepest divinity is where a man would least expect it: viz. in his colloquies in a dialogue between a butcher and a fishmonger.

JOHN FLORIO
1545–1625

John Florio was born in London in the beginning of the reign of King Edward VI, his father and mother flying from the Valtolin ('tis about Piedmont or Savoy) to London for religion: Waldenses.[37] The family is originally of Siena, where the name is to this day.

King Edward dying, upon the persecution of Queen Mary, they fled back again into their own country, where he was educated.

Afterwards he came into England, and was by King James made 'informator'[38] to Prince Henry for the Italian and French tongues, and clerk to the closet to Queen Anne.

He wrote *First* and *Second Fruits*, being two books of the instruction to learn the Italian tongue; *Dictionary*; and translated Montaigne's *Essays*.

He died of the great plague at Fulham in 1625.

THOMAS FULLER
1608–61

Thomas Fuller, DD, born at Orwincle in Northamptonshire. His father was minister there, and married one of the sisters of John Davenant, Bishop of Salisbury. – From Dr Edward Davenant.

He was a boy of pregnant wit, and when the bishop and his father were discoursing, he would be by and hearken, and now and then put in, and sometimes beyond expectation, or his years.

He was of a middle stature; strong set; curled hair; a very working head, in so much that, walking and meditating before dinner, he would eat up a penny loaf, not knowing that he did it. His natural memory was very great, to which he added the *art of memory*: he would repeat to you forwards and backwards all the signs from Ludgate to Charing Cross.

He was a fellow of Sydney College in Cambridge, where he wrote his *Divine Poems*. He was first minister of Broad Windsor in Dorset, and prebendary of the church of Salisbury. He was sequestered, being a royalist, and was afterwards minister of Waltham Abbey, and preacher of the Savoy, where he died, and is buried.

GEORGE HERBERT
1593–1633

Mr George Herbert was a kinsman (remote) and chaplain to Philip, Earl of Pembroke and Montgomery, and Lord Chamberlain. His lordship gave him a benefice at Bemmarton (between Wilton and Salisbury), a pitiful little chapel of ease to Foughelston. The old house was very ruinous. Here he built a very handsome house for the minister, of brick, and made a good garden and walks. He lies in the chancel, under no large, nor yet very good, marble gravestone, without any inscription.

He wrote sacred poems, called *The Church*, printed, Cambridge, 1633; a book entitled *The Country Parson*, not printed till about 1650. He also wrote a folio in Latin, which because the parson of Hineham could not read, his widow (then wife to Sir Robert Cooke) condemned to the uses of good housewifery.

He was buried (according to his own desire) with the singing service for the burial of the dead, by the singing men of Salisbury. Francis Sambroke (attorney) then assisted as a chorister boy; my uncle, Thomas Danvers, was at the funeral. Look in the register book at the office where he died, for the parish register is lost.

He married Jane, the third daughter of Charles Danvers, of Baynton in Wiltshire, but had no issue by her. He was a very fine complexion and consumptive. His marriage, I suppose, hastened his death. My kinswoman was a handsome wanton and ingenious.

When he was first married he lived a year or better at Dauntsey house. H. Allen, of Dauntsey, was well acquainted with him, who has told me that he had a very good hand on the lute, and that he set his own lyrics or sacred poems. 'Tis an honour to the place, to have had the heavenly and ingenious contemplation of this good man, who was pious even to prophesy:

Religion now on tiptoe stands,
Ready to go to the American strands.

THOMAS HOBBES
1588–1679

The writers of the lives of the ancient philosophers used to, in the first place, speak of their lineage, and they tell us that in process of time several great families accounted it their glory to be branched from such a wise man.

Why now should that method be omitted in this little history of our Malmesbury philosopher? Who though but of plebeian descent, his renown has and will give brightness to his name and family, which hereafter may arise glorious and flourish in riches and may justly take it an honour to be of kin to this worthy person, so famous for his learning, both at home and abroad.

Thomas Hobbes, then, whose life I write, was second son of Mr Thomas Hobbes, vicar of Westport next to Malmesbury, who married Middleton of Brockinborough (a yeomanly family). He was also vicar of Charlton (a mile hence): they are annexed, and both worth sixty or eighty pounds per annum.

Thomas, the father, was one of the ignorant 'Sir Johns' of Queen Elizabeth's time; could only read the prayers of the church and the homilies; and disesteemed learning (his son Edmund told me so), as not knowing the sweetness of it.

As to his father's ignorance and clownery, 'twas as good metal in the ore, which wants excoriating and refining. A wit requires much cultivation, much pains, and art and good conversation to perfect a man.

He had an elder brother whose name was Francis, a wealthy man and had been alderman of the borough; by profession a glover, which is a great trade here, and in times past much greater. Having no child, he contributed much to, or rather altogether maintained, his nephew Thomas at Magdalen Hall in Oxford; and when he died gave him a mowing ground called Gasten Ground, lying near to the horse fair, worth sixteen or eighteen pounds per annum; the rest of his lands he gave to his nephew Edmund.

Edmund was near two years elder than his brother Thomas, and something resembled him in aspect, not so tall, but fell much short of him in his intellect, though he was a good, plain, understanding country man. He had been bred at school with his brother, could have made theme and verse, and understood a little Greek to his dying day.

This Edmund had only one son named Francis, and two daughters married to country men (renters) in the neighbourhood. This Francis pretty well resembled his uncle Thomas, especially about the eye; and probably had he had good education might have been ingenious; but he drowned his wit in ale. He was left by his father and uncle Thomas eighty pounds or better per annum, but he was an ill husband. He died about two years after his father, and left five children.

Westport is the parish without the west gate (which is now demolished), which gate stood on the neck of land that joins Malmesbury to Westport. Here was, before the late wars, a very pretty church, consisting of three aisles, or rather a nave and two aisles (which took up the whole area), dedicated to St Mary; and fair spire-steeple, with five tuneable bells, which, when the town was taken (about 1644; ask William Aubrey) by Sir W. Waller, were converted into ordinance, and the church pulled down to the ground, that the enemy might not shelter themselves against the garrison. The steeple was higher than that now standing in the borough, which much added to the prospect. The windows were well painted, and in them were inscriptions that declared much antiquity; now here is rebuilt a church like a stable.

Thomas Hobbes of Malmesbury, philosopher, was born at his father's house in Westport, being that extreme house that points into, or faces, the horse fair; the furthest house on the left hand as you go to Tedbury, leaving the church on your right. To prevent mistakes, and that hereafter may rise no doubt what house was famous for this famous man's birth, I do here testify that in April 1659, his brother Edmund went with me into this house, and into the chamber where he was born. Now things begin to be antiquated, and I have heard some guess it might be at the house where his brother Edmund lived and died. But this is so, as I here deliver it. The house was given by Thomas, the vicar, to his daughter, whose daughter or granddaughter possessed it when I was there. It is a firm house, stone built and tiled, of one room (besides a buttery, or the like, within) below, and two chambers above. 'Twas in the innermost where he first drew breath.

The day of his birth was 5th April 1588, on a Friday morning, which that year was Good Friday. His mother fell in labour with him upon the fright of the invasion of the Spaniards –

At four years old he went to school in Westport Church, till eight; by that time he could read well, and number four figures. Afterwards he went to school to Malmesbury, to Mr Evans, the minister of the town; and afterwards to Mr Robert Latimer, a young man of about nineteen or twenty, newly come from the university, who then kept a private school in Westport, where the broad place is, next door north from the smith's shop, opposite to the Three Cups (as I take it). He was a bachelor and delighted in his scholar T.H.'s company, and used to instruct him, and two or three ingenious youths more, in the evening till nine o'clock. Here T.H. so well profited in his learning that at fourteen he went away a good school scholar to Magdalen Hall in Oxford. It is not to be forgotten, that before he went to university, he had turned Euripedes *Medea* out of Greek into Latin iambics, which he presented to his master. Mr H. told me that he would fain have had them, to have seen how he did grow. Twenty odd years ago I searched all old Mr Latimer's papers, but could not find them; the good housewives had sacrificed them.

I have heard his brother Edmund and Mr Wayte (his schoolfellow) say that when he was a boy he was playsome enough, but withal he had even then a contemplative melancholiness; he would get him into a corner, and learn his lesson by heart presently. His hair was black, and his schoolfellows were wont to call him 'crow'.

This Mr Latimer was a good Grecian, and the first that came into our parts hereabout since the Reformation. He was afterwards minister of Malmesbury, and from thence preferred to a better living of a hundred pounds per annum or more, at Leigh de la Mere within this hundred.

At Oxford Mr T.H. used, in the summer time especially, to rise very early in the morning, and would tie the leaden counters (which they used in those days at Christmas, at 'post and pair'[39]) with packthreads, which he did besmear with birdlime, and bait them with parings of cheese, and the jack-daws would spy them a vast distance up in the air, and as far as Osney Abbey, and strike at the bait, and so be entangled in the string, which the weight of the counter would make cling about their wings. He did not much care for logic, yet he learned it, and thought himself a good disputant. He took great delight there to go to the bookbinders' shops, and lie gaping on maps.

After he had taken his bachelor of arts degree, the then principal of Magdalen Hall (Sir James Hussey) recommended him to his young lord when he left Oxford, who had a conceit that he should profit more in his learning if he had a scholar of his own age to wait on him than if he had the information of a grave doctor. He was his lordship's page, and rode a-hunting and hawking with him, and kept his privy purse.

By this way of life he had almost forgotten his Latin; see Latin verses. He therefore brought him books of an Amsterdam print that he might carry in his pocket (particularly Caesar's *Commentaries*), which he did read in the lobby, or antechamber, whilst his lord was making his visits.

The Lord Chancellor Bacon loved to converse with him. He assisted his lordship in translating several of his essays into Latin, one, I well remember, is that *Of the Greatness of Cities*: the rest I have forgotten. His lordship was a very contemplative person, and was wont to contemplate in his delicious walks at Gorhambury, and dictate to Mr Thomas Bushell, or some other of his gentlemen, that attended him with ink and paper ready to set down his thoughts. His lordship would often say that he better liked Mr Hobbes's taking his thoughts, than any of the other, because he understood what he wrote, which the others not understanding, my lord would many times have a hard task to make sense of what they wrote.

It is to be remembered that about these times, Mr T.H. was much addicted to music, and practised on the bass viol.

1634: this summer – I remember 'twas in venison season (July or August) – Mr T.H. came into his native country to visit his friends, and amongst others he came then to see his old schoolmaster, Mr Robert Latimer at Leigh de la Mere, where I was then at school in the church, newly entered into my grammar by him. Here was the first place and time that ever I had the honour to see this worthy, learned man, who was then pleased to take notice of me, and the next day visited my relations. He was then a proper man, brisk, and in very good habit. His hair was then quite black. He stayed at Malmesbury and in the neighbourhood a week or better. 'Twas the last time that ever he was in Wiltshire.

He was forty years old before he looked on geometry, which happened accidentally. Being in a gentlemen's library, Euclid's *Elements* lay open, and 'twas the forty-seventh proposition in the first book. He read the proposition. 'By G—,' said he, 'this is impossible!' So he reads the demonstration of it, which referred him back to such a proposition, which proposition he read. That referred him back to another, which he also read. And so forth, that at last he was demonstratively convinced of that truth. This made him in love with geometry.

I have heard Sir Jonas Moore (and others) say that 'twas great pity he had not begun the study of the mathematics sooner, for such a working head would have made great advancement in it. So had he done, he would not have lain so open to his learned mathematical antagonists. But one may say of him, as one says of Joseph Scaliger,[40] that where he errs, he errs so ingeniously, that one had rather err with him than hit the mark with Clavius.[41] I have heard Mr Hobbes say that he was wont to draw lines on his thigh and on the sheets, abed, and also multiply and divide. He would often complain that algebra (though of great use) was too much admired, and so followed after, that it made men not contemplate and consider so much the nature and power of lines, which was a great hindrance to the growth of geometry; for that though algebra did rarely well and quickly, and easily in right lines, yet 'twould not *bite* in *solid* geometry.

Memorandum – after he began to reflect on the interest of the King of England as touching his affairs between him and the Parliament, for ten years together, his thoughts were much, or almost altogether, unhinged from the mathematics, but chiefly intent on his *De Cive*, and after that on his *Leviathan*: which was a great put-back to his mathematical improvement – for in ten years (or better) discontinuance of that study (especially) one's mathematics will become very rusty.

Memorandum – he told me that Bishop Mainwaring (of St David's) preached *his doctrine*; for which, among others, he was sent to the Tower. Then thought Mr Hobbes, 'tis time now for me to shift for myself, and so withdrew into France and resided at Paris. As I remember, there were others likewise did preach his doctrine. This little MS treatise grew to be his book *De Cive*, and at last grew there to be the so formidable *Leviathan*; the manner of writing of which book (he told me) was thus. He walked much and contemplated, and he had in the head of his staff a pen and inkhorn, carried always a notebook in his pocket, and as soon as a thought darted, he presently entered it into his book, or otherwise he might perhaps have lost it. He had drawn the design of the book into chapters, etc. so he knew whereabouts it would come in. Thus that book was made.

He wrote and published the *Leviathan* far from the intention either of disadvantage to His Majesty, or to flatter Oliver (who was not made Protector till three or four years after) on purpose to facilitate his return; for there is scarce a page in it that he does not upbraid him.

During his stay at Paris he went through a course of chemistry with Dr Davison; and he there also studied Vesalius' *Anatomy*. This I am sure was before 1648; for that Sir William Petty (then Dr Petty, physician) studied and dissected with him.

In 1650 or 1651 he returned into England, and lived most part in London, in Fetter Lane, where he wrote, or finished, his book *De Corpore*, in Latin and then in English; and wrote his lessons against the two Savilian professors at Oxford.

He was much in London till the restoration of His Majesty, having here convenience not only of books, but of learned conversation, as Mr John Selden, Dr William Harvey, John Vaughan, etc., whereof anon in the catalogue of his acquaintance.

I have heard him say, that at his lord's house in the country there was a good library, and books enough for him, and that his lordship stored the library with what books he thought fit to be bought; but he said, the want of learned conversation was a very great inconvenience, and that though he conceived he could order his thinking as well perhaps as another man, yet he found a great defect.

Amongst other of his acquaintances I must not forget our common friend, Mr Samuel Cowper, the prince of limners of this last age, who drew his picture as like as art could afford, and one of the best pieces he ever did: which His Majesty, at his return, bought of him, and conserves as one of his great rarities in his closet at Whitehall.

In 1659 his lord was – and some years before – at Little Salisbury House (now turned to the Middle Exchange) where he wrote, among other things, a poem, in Latin hexameter and pentameter, of the encroachment of the clergy (both Roman and reformed) on the civil power. I remember I saw then five hundred or more verses, for he numbered every tenth he wrote. I remember he did read Cluverius' *Historia Universalis* and made up his poem from thence. His amanuensis remembers this poem, for he wrote them out, but knows not what became of it.

His place of meditation was then in the portico in the garden.

His manner of thinking – he said that he sometimes would set his thoughts upon researching and contemplating always with this rule that he very much and deeply considered one thing at a time (that is, a week or a fortnight).

There was a report (and surely true) that in Parliament, not long after the king was settled, some of the bishops made a motion to have the good old gentleman burnt for a heretic. Which he hearing, feared that his papers might be searched by their order, and he told me that he had burned part of them. – I have received word from his amanuensis and executor that he 'remembers there were such verses for he wrote them out, but knows not what became of them, unless he presented them to Judge Vaughan, or burned them as I did seem to intimate'.

1660. The winter time of 1659 he spent in Derbyshire. In March following was the dawning of the coming in of our gracious sovereign, and in April the Aurora.[42]

I then sent a letter to him in the country to advertise him of the advent of his master the king and desired him by all means to be in London before his arrival; and knowing His Majesty was a great lover of good painting I must needs presume he could not but suddenly see Mr Cowper's curious pieces, of whose fame he had so much heard abroad and seen some of his work, and likewise that he would sit to him for his picture, at which place and time he would have the best convenience of renewing His Majesty's graces to him. He returned me thanks for my friendly intimation and came to London in May following.

It happened, about two and three days after His Majesty's happy return, that, as he was passing in his coach through the Strand, Mr Hobbes was standing at Little Salisbury House gate (where his lord then lived). The king espied him, put off his hat very kindly to him, and asked him how he did. About a week after, he had oral conference with His Majesty at Mr S. Cowper's, where, as he sat for his picture, he was diverted by Mr Hobbes's pleasant discourse. Here His Majesty's favours were renewed to him, and order was given that he should have free access to His Majesty, who was always much delighted in his wit and smart repartees.

The wits at the court were wont to bait him. But he feared none of them, and would make his part good. The king would call him 'the bear'. 'Here comes the bear to be baited!'

Repartees. He was marvellous happy and ready in his replies, and that without rancour (except provoked) – but now I speak of his readiness in replies as to wit and drollery. He would say that he was not afraid to give, neither was he adroit at, a present answer to a serious query: he had as lief they should have expected an extemporary solution to an arithmetical problem, for he turned and winded and compounded in philosophy, politics, etc. as if he had been at analytical work. He always avoided, as much as he could, to conclude hastily.

Memorandum – from 1660 till the time he last went into Derbyshire, he spent most of his time in London at his lord's (viz. at Little Salisbury House, then Queen Street, lastly Newport House), following his contemplation and study. He contemplated and invented (set down a hint with a pencil or so) in the morning, but compiled in the afternoon.

In 1664 I said to him, 'Methinks 'tis pity that you that have such a clear reason and working head did never take into consideration the learning of the laws;' and I endeavoured to persuade him to it. But he answered that he was not like enough to have life enough left to go through with such a long and difficult task. I then presented him the Lord Chancellor

Bacon's *Elements of the Law* (a thin quarto) in order thereunto and to draw him on, which he was pleased to accept, and perused; and the next time I came to him he showed me therein two flawed arguments in the second page, which I am heartily sorry are now out of my remembrance.

1665. This year he told me he was willing to do some good to the town where he was born; that His Majesty loved him well and if I could find out something in our country[43] that was in his gift, he did believe he could beg it of His Majesty, and seeing he was bred a scholar, he thought it most proper to endow a free school there, which is wanting *now* (for before the reformation, all monasteries had great schools appended to them, e.g. Magdalen School and New College School). After enquiry I found out a piece of land in Bradon Forest (of about twenty-five pounds per annum value) that was in His Majesty's gift, which he designed to have obtained from His Majesty for a salary for a schoolmaster; but the queen's priests, smelling out the design and being his enemies, hindered this public and charitable intention.

1675. He left London with no intention of returning, and spent the remainder of his days in Derbyshire with the Earl of Devonshire at Chatsworth and Hardwick, in contemplation and study.

His complexion. In his youth he was unhealthy and of an ill complexion (yellowish).

His lord, who was a waster, sent him up and down to borrow money, and to get gentlemen to be bound for him, being ashamed to speak himself. He took colds, being wet in his feet (then were no hackney coaches to stand in the streets), and trod both his shoes aside in the same way. Notwithstanding he was well beloved: they loved his company for his pleasant facetiousness and good nature.

From forty, or better, he grew healthier and then he had a fresh, ruddy complexion. He would say that 'there might be good wits of all complexions; but good-natured, impossible.'

Head. In his old age he was very bald (which claimed a veneration); yet within door, he used to study, and sit, bare-headed, and said he never took cold in his head but that the greatest trouble was to keep off the flies from pitching on the baldness.

Skin. His skin was soft and of that kind which my Lord Chancellor Bacon in his *History of Life and Death* calls a goose skin, i.e. of a wide texture –

A wide skin, a wide scull, a wide wit.

Face not very great; ample forehead; whiskers yellowish-reddish, which naturally turned up – which is a sign of a brisk wit.

Beard. Below he was shaved close, except a little tip under his lip. Not that but nature could have afforded a venerable beard, but being naturally of a cheerful and pleasant humour, he affected not at all austerity and gravity and to look severe. He desired not the reputation of his wisdom to be taken from the cut of his beard, but from his reason –

A beard does not make a philosopher. 'He consists of no more than the point of his beard and his two moustaches; as a result all that is needed to destroy him is three scissor cuts.'[44]

Eye. He had a good eye, and that of a hazel colour, which was full of life and spirit, even to the last. When he was earnest in discourse, there shone (as it were) a bright live coal within it. He had two kinds of looks – when he laughed, was witty, and in a merry humour one could scarce see his eyes; by and by, when he was serious and positive, he opened his eyes round (i.e. his eyelids). He had middling eyes, not big, nor very little.

Stature. He was six foot high, and something better, and went indifferently erect, or rather, considering his great age, very erect.

Sight; wit. His sight and wit continued to the last. He had a curious sharp sight, as he had a sharp wit which was also so sure and steady (and contrary to that men call 'broad-wittedness') that I have heard him oftentimes say that in multiplying and dividing he never mistook a figure: and so in other things.

He thought much and with excellent method and steadiness, which made him seldom make a false step.

His books. He had very few books. I never saw above half a dozen about him in his chamber. Homer and Virgil were commonly on his table; sometimes Xenophon, or some probable history, and Greek Testament, or so.

Reading. He had read much, if one considers his long life; but his contemplation was much more than his reading. He was wont to say that if he had read as much as other men, he should have known no more than other men.

His physic. He seldom used any physic. What 'twas I have forgotten, but will enquire of Mr Shelbrooke his apothecary at the Black Spread Eagle in The Strand.

Memorandum – Mr Hobbes was very sick and like to die at Bristol House in Queen Street, about 1668.

He was wont to say that he had rather have the advice, or take physic from an experienced old woman, that had been at many sick people's bedsides, than from the most learned but inexperienced physician.

Temperance and diet. He was, even in his youth, generally temperate, both as to wine and women.

I have heard him say that he did believe he had been in excess in his life, a hundred times; which, considering his great age, did not amount to above once a year. When he did drink, he would drink to excess to have the benefit of vomiting, which he did easily; by which benefit neither his wit was disturbed longer than he was spewing nor his stomach oppressed; but he never was, nor could not endure to be, habitually a good fellow, i.e. to drink every day wine with company, which, though not to drunkenness, spoils the brain.

For his last thirty years or more his diet, etc. was very moderate and regular. After sixty he drank no wine, his stomach grew weak, and he did eat most fish, especially whitings, for he said he digested fish better than flesh. He rose about seven, had his breakfast of bread and butter; and took his walk, meditating till ten; then he did put down the minutes of his thoughts, which he penned in the afternoon.

He had an inch thick board about sixteen inches square, whereon paper was pasted. On this board he drew his lines (schemes). When a line came into his head, he would, as he was walking, take a rude memorandum of it, to preserve it in his memory till he came to his chamber. He was never idle; his thoughts were always working.

His dinner was provided for him exactly by eleven, for he could not now stay till his lord's hour – that is, about two. That his stomach could not bear.

After dinner he took a pipe of tobacco, and then threw himself immediately on his bed, with his band off, and slept (took a nap of about half an hour).

In the afternoon he penned his morning thoughts.

Exercises. Besides his daily walking, he did twice or thrice a year play tennis (at about seventy-five he did it); then went to bed there and was well rubbed. This he did believe would make him live two or three years longer.

In the country, for want of a tennis court, he would walk uphill and downhill in the park till he was in a great sweat, and then give the servant some money to rub him.

Prudence. He gave to his amanuensis, James Wheldon (the Earl of Devon's baker, who writes a delicate hand), his pension at Leicester, yearly, to wait on him, and take care of him, which he did perform to him living and dying, with great respect and diligence: for which consideration he made him his executor.

Habit. In cold weather he commonly wore a black velvet coat, lined with fur; if not, some other coat so lined. But all the year he wore a kind of boots of Spanish leather, laced or tied along the sides with black ribbons.

Singing. He had always books of written music lying on his table – e.g. of H. Lawes' *Songs* – which at night, when he was abed, and the doors made fast, and was sure nobody heard him, he sang aloud (not that he had a very good voice) but for his health's sake: he did believe it did his lungs good, and conduced much to prolong his life.

Shaking palsy. He had the shaking palsy in his hands, which began in France before the year 1650, and has grown upon him by degrees, ever since, so that he has not been able to write very legibly since 1665 or 1666, as I find by some of his letters to me.

Charity. His brotherly love to his kindred has already been spoken of. He was very charitable according to his means to those that were true objects of his bounty. One time, I remember, going in The Strand, a poor and infirm man craved his alms. He, beholding him with eyes of pity and compassion, put his hand in his pocket, and gave 6d. Said a divine (that is Dr Jasper Mayne) that stood by, 'Would you have done this, if it had not been Christ's command?' 'Yea,' said he. 'Why?' said the other. 'Because,' said he, 'I was in pain to consider the miserable condition of the old man; and now my alms, giving him some relief, does also ease me.'

Aspersions and envy. His work was attended with envy, which threw several aspersions and false reports on him. For instance, one (common) was that he was afraid to lie alone at night in his chamber (I have often heard him say that he was not afraid of the *sprites*, but afraid of being knocked on the head for five or ten pounds, which rogues might think he had in his chamber); and several other tales, as untrue.

I have heard some positively affirm that he had a yearly pension from the King of France – possibly for having asserted such a monarchy as the King of France exercises, but for what other grounds I know not, unless it be for that the present King of France is reputed an encourager of choice and able men in all faculties who can contribute to his greatness. I never heard him speak of any such thing, and since his death, I have enquired of his most intimate friends in Derbyshire, who write to me they never heard of any such thing. Had it been so, he, nor they, ought to have been ashamed of it, and it had been becoming the munificence of so great a prince to have done it.

Atheism. For his being branded with atheism, his writings and virtuous life testify against it. That he was a Christian 'tis clear, for he received the sacrament of Dr John Pierson, and in his confession to Dr John Cosins, on his (as he thought) deathbed, declared that he liked the religion of the Church of England best of all other.

He would have the worship of God performed with music (he told me).

'Tis of custom in the lives of wise men to put down their sayings. Now if truth (uncommon) delivered clearly and wittily may go for a saying, his common discourse was full of them, and which for the most part were sharp and significant.

Thomas Hobbes said that if it were not for the gallows, some men are of so cruel a nature as to take a delight in killing men more than I should to kill a bird.

I have heard him inveigh much against the cruelty of Moses for putting so many thousands to the sword for bowing to the golden calf.

I have heard him say that Aristotle was the worst teacher that ever was, the worst politician and ethic – a country fellow that could live in the world would be as good: but his rhetoric and discourse of animals was rare.

Insert the love verses he made not long before his death:

1.

Tho' I am now past ninety, and too old
T'expect preferment in the court of Cupid,
And many winters made me even so cold
I am become almost all over stupid,

2.

Yet I can love and have a mistress too,
As fair as can be and as wise as fair;
And yet not proud, nor anything will do
To make me of her favour to despair.

3.

To tell her who she is were very bold;
But if i' th' character your self you find
Think not the man a fool tho' he be old
Who loves in body fair a fairer mind.

Catalogue of his learned familiar friends and acquaintances. [45]

Mr Benjamin Jonson, Poet Laureate, was his loving and familiar friend and acquaintance.

Sir Robert Aiton, Scoto-Britannus, a good poet and critic and good scholar. He was nearly related to his lord's lady (Bruce). And he desired Ben Jonson, and this gentleman, to give their judgement on his style of his translation of Thucydides. He lies buried in Westminster Abbey, and has there an elegant monument and inscription.

Lucius Cary, Lord Falkland was his great friend and admirer and so was *Sir William Petty*; both which I have here enrolled amongst those friends I have heard him speak of, but Dr Blackburne left 'em both out (to my admiration). I asked him why he had done so? He answered because they were both unknown to foreigners.

When he was at Florence he contracted a friendship with *Galileo Galileo*, whom he extremely venerated and magnified; and not only as he was a prodigious wit, but for his sweetness and manners. They pretty well resembled one another as to their countenances, as by their pictures does appear; were both cheerful and melancholic-sanguine; and had both a consimility of fate, to be hated and persecuted by the ecclesiastics.

Descartes and he were acquainted and mutually respected one another. He would say that had he kept himself to geometry, he had been the best geometer in the world but that his head did not lie for philosophy.

Sir William Petty (of Ireland), Fellow of the Royal Society, a person of stupendous invention and of as great prudence and humanity, had high esteem of him. His acquaintance began at Paris, 1648 or 1649, at which time Mr Hobbes studied Vesalius' *Anatomy*, and Sir William with him. He then assisted Mr Hobbes in drawing his schemes for his book of optics, for he had a very fine hand in those days for drawing, which drafts Mr Hobbes did much commend. His faculty in this kind conciliated them sooner to the familiarity of our common friend.

Mr S. Cowper aforesaid, at whose house they often met. – He drew his picture twice: the first the king has, the other is yet in the custody of his widow; but he gave it, indeed, to me (and I promised I would give it to the archives at Oxford, with a short inscription on the back side, as a monument of his friendship to me and ours to Mr Hobbes – *sed haec omnia inter nos*[46]) but I, like a fool, did not take possession of it, for something of the garment was not quite finished, and he died, I being then in the country – *sed hoc non ad rem.*[47]

Mr Abraham Cowley, the poet, who has bestowed on him an immortal Pindaric ode, which is in his poems.

William Harvey, doctor of physic and surgery, inventor of the circulation of the blood, who left him in his will ten pounds, as his brother told me at his funeral.

Mr Edmund Waller of Beaconsfield was his great friend, and acquainted at Paris – I believe before.

When his *Leviathan* came out, he sent by his stationer's man (Andrew Crooke) a copy of it, well bound, to *Mr John Selden* in the Carmelite Buildings. Mr Selden told the servant he did not know Mr Hobbes, but had heard much of his worth, and that he should be very glad to be acquainted with him. Whereupon Mr Hobbes waited on him. From which time there was a strict friendship between them to his dying day. He left by his will to Mr Hobbes a legacy of ten pounds.

Sir John Vaughan, Lord Chief Justice of the Common Pleas, was his great acquaintance, to whom he made visits three times or more in a week – out of term in the mornings, in term time in the afternoons.

Sir Jonas Moore, mathematician, surveyor of His Majesty's ordnance, who had great veneration for Mr Hobbes, and was wont much to lament he fell to study of the mathematics so late.

To conclude, he had a high esteem for the Royal Society, having said that 'Natural Philosophy was removed from the universities to Gresham College', meaning the Royal Society that meets there; and the Royal Society (generally) had the like for him: and he would long since have been ascribed a member there, but for the sake of one or two persons, whom he took to be his enemies. In their meeting at Gresham College in his picture, drawn by the life, 1663, by a good hand, which they much esteem, and several copies have been taken of it.

BEN JONSON
1574-1637

Mr Benjamin Jonson, Poet Laureate; I remember when I was a scholar at Trinity College, Oxford, 1646, I heard Dr Ralph Bathurst (now Dean of Wells) say that Ben Jonson was a Warwickshire man – ask about this. 'Tis agreed that his father was a minister; and by his epistle dedicatory of *Every Man in his Humour* to Mr William Camden, that he was a Westminster scholar and that Mr W. Camden was his schoolmaster.

Anthony Wood in his *History* says he was born in Westminster: that (at riper years) after he had studied at Cambridge he came of his own accord to Oxford and there entered himself in Christ Church and took his Master's degree in Oxford (or it was conferred on him) in 1619.

His mother, after his father's death, married a bricklayer; and 'tis generally said that he wrought some time with his stepfather (and particularly on the garden wall of Lincoln's Inn next to Chancery Lane – from old parson Richard Hill of Stretton, Herefordshire, 1646), and that a knight, a bencher,[48] walking through and hearing him repeat some Greek verses out of Homer, discoursing with him, and finding him to have a wit extraordinary, gave him some exhibition to maintain him at Trinity College in Cambridge.

Then he went into the Low Countries, and spent some time (not very long) in the army, not to the disgrace of himself, as you may find in his *Epigrams*.

Then he came over into England, and acted and wrote, but both ill, at the Green Curtain, a kind of nursery or obscure playhouse, somewhere in the suburbs (I think towards Shoreditch or Clerkenwell) – from J. Greenhill.

Then he undertook again to write a play, and did hit it admirably well, viz. *Every Man in his Humour*, which was his first good one.

Sergeant John Hoskins, of Herefordshire, was his *father*. I remember his son (Sir Bennet Hoskins, baronet, who was something poetical in his youth) told me, that when he desired to be adopted his son: 'No,' said he, ''tis honour enough for me to be your brother; I am your father's son, 'twas he that polished me, I do acknowledge it.'

He was (or rather had been) of a clear and fair skin; his habit was very plain. I have heard Mr Lacy, the player, say that he was wont to wear a coat like a coachman's coat, with slits under the armpits. He would many times exceed in drink (Canary was his beloved liquor): then he would tumble home to bed, and, when he had thoroughly perspired, then to study. I have seen his studying chair, which was of straw, such as old women used, and as Aulus Gellius[49] is drawn in.

When I was in Oxford, Bishop Skinner (of Oxford), who lay at our college, was wont to say that he understood an author as well as any man in England.

He mentions in his *Epigrams* a son that he had, and his epitaph.

Long since, in King James's time, I have heard my Uncle Danvers say that he lived without Temple Bar, at a comb-maker's shop, about the Elephant and Castle. In his later time he lived in Westminster, in the house under which you pass as you go out of the churchyard into the old palace; where he died.

He lies buried in the north aisle in the path of square stone (the rest is lozenge), opposite to the scutcheon of Robertus de Ros, with this inscription only on him, in a pavement square, of blue marble, about fourteen inches square:

O RARE BENN IOHNSON

which was done at the charge of Jack Young (afterwards knighted) who, walking there when the grave was covering, gave the fellow eighteen pence to cut it.

His motto before his (bought) books was *Tanquam Explorator*.[50] I remember 'tis in Seneca's *Epistles*.

He was a favourite of the Lord Chancellor Egerton, as appears by several verses to him. In one he begs his lordship to do a friend of his a favour.

'Twas an ingenious remark of my Lady Hoskins, that B.J. never writes of love, or if he does, does it not naturally.

He killed Mr Marlowe, the poet, on Bunhill, coming from the Green Curtain playhouse. – From Sir Edward Shirburn.

Ben Jonson had fifty pounds per annum for many years together to keep off Sir W. Wiseman of Essex from being sheriff. At last King James pricked him,[51] and Ben came to His Majesty and told him he 'had pricked him to the heart' and then explained himself (meaning Sir W. W. being pricked sheriff) and got him struck off.

See his *Execration at Vulcan*. See *None-such-Charles*. When B.J. was dying King Charles sent him but ten pounds. Ask T. Shadwell for notes of B.J. from the Duke of Newcastle; and also ask Thomas Henshawe (as also about the stones in Ireland). Ask my Lord Clifford of the gentleman that cut the grass under Ben Jonson's feet, of whom he said, 'Ungrateful man! I showed him Juvenal.'

Ben Jonson had one eye lower than the other and bigger. He took a catalogue from Mr Lacy (the player) of the Yorkshire dialect. 'Twas his hint for clownery to his comedy called *The Tale of the Tub*. This I had from Mr Lacy.

King James made him write against the Puritans, who began to be troublesome in his time.

A grace by Ben Jonson, *extempore*, before King James:

Our King and Queen, the Lord-God blesse,
The Paltzgrave, and the Lady Besse,
And God blesse every living thing
That lives, and breath's, and loves the King.
God bless the Council of Estate,
And Buckingham, the fortunate.
God blesse them all, and keep them safe,
And God blesse me, and God blesse Raph.

The King was mighty inquisitive to know who this Raph was. Ben told him 'twas the drawer at the Swan Tavern, by Charing Cross, who drew him good Canary. For this drollery His Majesty gave him a hundred pounds.

This account I received from Mr Isaac Walton (who wrote Dr John Donne's Life), 2nd December, 1680, he being then eighty-seven years of age. This is his own handwriting.

I hardly knew Ben Jonson: but my Lord of Winchester knew him very well, and says he was in the sixth, that is the uppermost form in Westminster school. At which time his father died, and his mother married a bricklayer, who made him (much against his will) to help him in his trade. But in a short time, his schoolmaster, Mr Camden, got him a better employment, which was to attend or accompany a son of Walter Raleigh's in his travails. Within a short time after their return, they parted (I think not in cool blood), and with a love matching what they had in their travails (not to be commended); and then, Ben began to set up for himself in the trade by which he got his subsistence and fame. Of which I need not give any account. He got in time to have a hundred pounds a year from the king, also, a pension from the city, and the like from many of the nobility, and some of the gentry, which was well paid for love or fear that of his railing in verse or prose, or both. My Lord of Winchester told me, he told him he was (in his long retirement, and sickness, when he saw him, which was often) much afflicted that he had profaned the scripture, in his plays; and lamented it with horror; yet, that at that time of his long retirement, his pensions (so much as came in) were given to a woman that governed him, with whom he lived and died near the Abbey in Westminster; and that neither she nor he took much care for the next week; and would be sure not to want wine; of which he usually took too much before he went to bed, if not oftener and sooner. My lord tells me, he knows not, but thinks he was born in Westminster. The question may be put to Mr Wood very easily upon what grounds he is positive as to his being born there. He is a friendly man and will resolve it. So much for brave Ben.

RICHARD LOVELACE
1618–58

Richard Lovelace, esq.: he was a most beautiful gentleman.

Geminum, seu lumina, sydus,
Et dignos Baccho digitos, et Apolline crines,
Impubesque genas, et eburnea colla, decusque
Oris, et in niveo mistum candore ruborem.[52]

He died in a cellar in Long Acre, a little before the restoration of His Majesty. Mr Edmund Wyld, etc. have made collections for him, and given him money.

One of the handsomest men in England. He was of Kent, had five hundred pounds per annum and more (ask E. W.).

He was an extraordinarily handsome man, but proud. He wrote a poem called *Lucasta*, octavo, printed in London by Thomas Harper to be sold at the Gun in Ivy Lane, 1649.

He was of Gloucester Hall, as I have been told.

He had two younger brothers, viz. Colonel Francis Lovelace, and another brother (William) that died at Carmarthen.

George Petty, haberdasher, in Fleet Street, carried twenty shillings to him every Monday morning from Sir Many and Charles Cotton, esq., for many months, but was never repaid.

ANDREW MARVELL
1621–78

Mr Andrew Marvell: his father was minister of, I think, Hull (ask).

He had good grammar education, and was after sent to Cambridge.

In the time of Oliver the Protector he was Latin secretary. He was a great master of the Latin tongue; and excellent poet in Latin or English: for Latin verses there was no man could come into competition with him. The verses called *The Advice to the Painter* were of his making.

His native town of Hull loved him so well that they elected him for their representative in Parliament, and gave him an honourable pension to maintain him.

He was of middling stature, pretty strong set, roundish face, cherry cheeked, hazel eye, brown hair. He was in his conversation very modest, and of very few words: and though he loved wine he would never drink hard in company, and was wont to say that 'he would not play the good fellow in any man's company in whose hands he would not trust his life'.

He kept bottles of wine at his lodging, and many times he would drink liberally by himself to refresh his spirits, and exalt his muse. I remember I have been told (Mr Haake and Dr Pell) that a learned High-German was wont to keep bottles of good Rhenish wine in his study, and when he had spent his spirits, he would drink a good rummer of it.

James Harrington, esq. (author of *Oceana*), was his intimate friend. John Pell, DD, was one of his acquaintances. He had not a general acquaintance.

He died in London on the 18th August, 1678, and is buried in St Giles church in-the-fields about the middle (ask) of the south aisle. Some suspect that he was poisoned by the Jesuits, but I cannot be positive.

I remember I heard him say that the Earl of Rochester was the only man in England that had the true vein of satire.

JOHN MILTON
1608–74

Mr John Milton was of an Oxfordshire family.

His grandfather (a Roman Catholic), of Holton, in Oxfordshire, near Shotover.

His father was brought up in the University of Oxford, at Christ Church, and his grandfather disinherited him because he kept not to the Catholic religion. So thereupon he came to London, and became a scrivener (brought up by a friend of his; was not an apprentice), and got plentiful estate by it, and left it off many years before he died. He was an ingenious man; delighted in music; composed many songs now in print, especially that of *Oriana*.

I have been told that his father composed a song of fourscore parts for the Lantgrave of Hess, for which his highness sent a medal of gold, or a noble present. He died about 1647; buried in Cripplegate church, from his house in the Barbican.

His son John was born in Bread Street, in London, at the Spread Eagle, which was his house (he had also in that street another house, the Rose; and other houses in other places).

John Milton was born on the 9th December, 1608, half an hour after six in the morning.

In 1619, he was ten years old, as by his picture; and was then a poet.

His schoolmaster then was a Puritan in Essex, who cut his hair short.

He went to school to old Mr Gill at St Paul's School. Went, at his own charge only, to Christ's College in Cambridge at fifteen, where he stayed eight years at least. Then he travelled into France and Italy (he had Sir H. Wotton's commendatory letters). At Geneva he contracted a great friendship with the learned Dr Deodati of Geneva – see his poems. He was acquainted with Sir Henry Wotton, ambassador at Venice, who delighted in his company. He was several years beyond sea, and returned to England just upon the breaking out of the Civil Wars.

From his brother, Christopher Milton – when he went to school, when he was very young, he studied very hard, and sat up very late, commonly till twelve or one o'clock at night, and his father ordered the maid to sit up for him, and in those years (ten) he composed many copies of verses that might well become a riper age. And was a very hard student in the university, and performed all his exercises there with very good applause.

His first tutor there was Mr Chapell; from whom receiving some unkindness, he was afterwards (though it seemed contrary to the rules of the college) transferred to the tuition of one Mr Tovell, who died parson of Lutterworth.

He went to travel about the year 1638 and was abroad about a year's space, chiefly in Italy.

Immediately after his return he took a lodging at Mr Russell's, a tailor, in St Bride's churchyard, and took into tuition his sister's two sons, Edward and John Phillips, the first ten, the other nine years of age; and in a year's time made them capable of interpreting a Latin author at sight, etc. And within the three years they went through the best of Latin and Greek poets – Lucretius and Manilius of the Latins; Hesiod, Aratus, Dionysius Afer, Oppian, Apollonii *Argonautica* and Quintus Calaber. Cato, Varro and Columella *De re rustica* were the very first authors they learnt. As he was severe on one hand, so he was most familiar and free in his conversation to those to whom he was most sour in his way of education.

NB He made his nephews songsters, and sing, from the time they were with him.

He married his first wife Mary Powell of Fost Hill at Shotover, in Oxfordshire, by whom he had four children. He has two daughters living: Deborah was his amanuensis (he taught her Latin and to read Greek to him when he had lost his eyesight).

She went from him to her mother's in the king's quarters near Oxford; and wrote the *Triplechord* about divorce.

Two opinions do not well on the same bolster. She was a royalist, and went to her mother to the king's quarters, near Oxford. I have perhaps so much charity to her that she might not wrong his bed: but what man, especially contemplative, would like to have a young wife environed and stormed by the sons of Mars, and those of the enemy party?

His first wife (Mrs Powell, a royalist) was brought up and lived where there was a great deal of company and merriment. And when she came to live with her husband, at Mr Russell's, in St Bride's churchyard, she found it very solitary; no company came to her; oftentimes heard his nephews beaten and cry. This life was irksome to her, and so she went to her parents at Fost Hill. He sent for her, after some time; and I think his servant was evilly entreated: but as for matter of wronging his bed, I never heard the least suspicions; nor had he, of that, any jealousy.

He had a middle wife, whose name was (he thinks Katherine) Woodcock. No child living by her.

He married his second[53] wife, Elizabeth Minshull, the year before the sickness:[54] a genteel person, a peaceful and agreeable humour.

He was Latin secretary to the Parliament.

His sight began to fail him at first upon his writing against Salmasius, and before 'twas fully completed one eye absolutely failed. Upon the writing of the other books, after that, his other eye decayed.

His eyesight was decaying about twenty years before his death: ask, when stark blind? His father read without spectacles at eighty-four. His mother had very weak eyes, and used spectacles presently after she was thirty years old.

After he was blind he wrote these following books: *Paradise Lost*, *Paradise Regained*, *Grammar*, *Dictionary* (imperfect) – ask if there were more.

I heard that after he was blind that he was writing a Latin Dictionary (in the hand of Moyses Pitt[55]). His widow states she gave all his papers (among which this dictionary, imperfect) to his nephew, a sister's son that he brought up, Phillips, who lives near the Maypole in the Strand (ask). She has a great many letters by her from learned men, his acquaintances, both of England and beyond sea.

He lived in several places, e.g. Holborn near King's Gate. He died in Bunhill, opposite to the artillery-garden wall.

He died of the gout struck in, the 9th or 10th November, 1674, as appears by his apothecary's book.

He lies buried in St Giles's Cripplegate, upper end of the chancel at the right hand, see his gravestone. Memorandum – his stone is now removed; for about two years since (now, 1681), the two steps to the communion table were raised. I guess John Speed and he lie together.

His harmonical and ingenious soul did lodge in a beautiful and well proportioned body:

In toto nusquam corpore menda fuit.[56]

He was a spare man. He was scarce so tall as I am – ask how many feet I am high: answer, of middle stature.

He had brown hair. His complexion exceeding fair – he was so fair that they called him 'the lady of Christ's College'. Oval face. His eye a dark grey.

He had a delicate tuneable voice, and had good skill. His father instructed him. He had an organ in his house: he played on that most.

Of a very cheerful humour. – He would be cheerful even in his gout fits, and sing.

He was very healthy and free from all diseases: seldom took any physic (only sometimes he took manna): only towards his latter end he was visited with the gout, spring and fall.

He had a very good memory; but I believe that his excellent method of thinking and disposing did much to help his memory.

He pronounced the letter R (*littera canina)* very hard – a certain sign of a satirical wit – from John Dryden.

Write his name in red letters on his pictures, with his widow, to preserve.

His widow has his picture, drawn very well and like, when a Cambridge scholar.

She has his picture when a Cambridge scholar, which ought to be engraven; for the pictures before his books are not *at all* like him.

His exercise was chiefly walking.

He was an early riser (that is at 4 o'clock in the morning); yea, after he lost his sight. He had a man read to him. The first thing he read was a Hebrew Bible, and that was at half past four. Then he contemplated.

At seven his man came to him again, and then read to him again, and wrote till dinner: the writing was as much as the reading. His second daughter, Deborah, could read to him Latin, Italian and French, and Greek. She married in Dublin to one Mr Clarke (sells silk, etc.); very like her father. The other sister is Mary, more like her mother.

After dinner he used to walk three or four hours at a time (he always had a garden where he lived); went to bed about nine.

Temperate man, rarely drank between meals.

Extremely pleasant in his conversation, and at dinner, supper, etc., but satirical.

From Mr E. Phillips – All the time of writing his *Paradise Lost*, his vein began at the autumnal equinoctial, and ceased at the vernal (or thereabouts: I believe about May): and this was four or five years of his doing it. He began about two years before the king came in, and finished about three years after the king's restoration.

In the fourth book of *Paradise Lost* there are about six verses of Satan's exclamation to the sun, which Mr E. Phillips remembers about fifteen or sixteen years before ever his poem was thought of. Which verses were intended for the beginning of a tragedy that he had designed, but was diverted from it by other business.

Whatever he wrote against monarchy was out of no animosity to the king's person, or out of any faction or interest, but out of a pure zeal to the liberty of mankind, which he thought would be greater under a free state than under a monarchical government. His being so conversant in Livy and the Roman authors, and the greatness he saw done by the Roman commonwealth, and the virtue of their great commanders induced him to.

From Mr Abraham Hill. Memorandum – his sharp writing against Alexander More, of Holland, upon a mistake, notwithstanding he had given him by the ambassador all satisfaction to the contrary: viz. that book called *Clamor* written by Peter du Moulin. Well, that was all one; he having written it, it should go into the world; one of them was as bad as the other.

Mr John Milton made two admirable panegyrics, as to sublimity of wit, one on Oliver Cromwell, and the other on Thomas, Lord Fairfax, both of which his nephew Mr Phillips has. But he has hung back these two years, as to imparting copies to me for the collection of mine with you. Wherefore I desire you in your next to intimate your desire of having these two copies of verses aforesaid. Were they made in commendation of the devil, 'twere all one to me: 'tis the ethos that I look after. I have been told 'tis beyond Waller's or anything in that kind.

He was visited much by learned men; more than he did desire.

He was mightily importuned to go into France and Italy. Foreigners came much to see him, and much admired him, and offered to him great preferment to come over to them: and that the only inducement of several foreigners that came over into England, was chiefly to see Oliver Protector, and Mr John Milton; and would see the house and the chamber where *he* was born. He was much more admired abroad than at home.

His familiar learned acquaintances were Mr Andrew Marvell, Mr Skinner, Dr Pagett, MD; Mr Skinner, who was his disciple; John Dryden, esq., Poet Laureate, who very much admires him, and went to him to have leave to put his *Paradise Lost* into a drama in rhyme. Mr Milton received him civilly, and told him he would give him leave to tag his verses.

His widow assures me that Mr T. Hobbes was not one of his acquaintances, that her husband did not like him at all, but he would acknowledge him to be a man of great parts, and a learned man. Their interests and tenets did run counter to each other: see in Hobbes's *Behemoth*.

SIR THOMAS MORE
1480–1535

Sir Thomas More, Lord Chancellor – his country house was at Chelsea in Middlesex, where Sir John Danvers built his house. The chimney piece of marble in St John's chamber was the chimney piece of Sir Thomas More's chamber, as Sir John himself told me. Where the gate is now, adorned with two noble pyramids, there stood anciently a gatehouse, which was flat on the top, leaded, from whence is a most pleasant prospect of the Thames and the fields beyond. On this place the Lord Chancellor More was wont to recreate himself and contemplate. It happened one time that a Tom of Bedlam came up to him and had a mind to have thrown him from the battlements, saying 'Leap, Tom, leap.' The Chancellor was in his gown, and besides ancient, and not able to struggle with such a strong fellow. My lord had a little dog with him; said he 'Let us first throw the dog down, and see what sport that will be;' so the dog was thrown over. 'This is very fine sport,' said my lord, 'let us fetch him up, and try once more.' While the madman was going down, my lord fastened the door, and called for help, but ever after kept the door shut.

Memorandum – that in his *Utopia* his law is that the young people are to see each other stark-naked before marriage. Sir William Roper, of Eltham in Kent, came one morning, pretty early, to my lord, with a proposal to marry one of his daughters. My lord's daughters were then both together a bed in a truckle bed in their father's chamber asleep. He carries Sir William into the chamber and takes the sheet by the corner and suddenly whips it off. Here was all the trouble of the wooing. – This account I had from my honoured friend old Mrs Tyndale, whose grandfather Sir William Stafford was an intimate acquaintance of this Sir William Roper, who told him the story.

This Sir William Roper (from whom is descended the Lord Tenham) had in one piece, drawn by Hans Holbein, the pictures of Sir Thomas More, his lady and all his children, which hung at his house aforesaid in Kent: but about 1675 'twas presented as a rarity to King Charles II and hangs in Whitehall.

His discourse was extraordinarily facetious. Riding one night, upon the sudden he crossed himself with a great cross, crying out 'Jesu Maria! do not you see that prodigious dragon in the sky?' They all looked up, and one did not see it, nor the other did not see it. At length one had spied it, and at last all had spied. Whereas there was no such phantom; only he imposed on their fantasies.

After he was beheaded, his trunk was interred in Chelsea church, near the middle of the south wall, where was some slight monument erected, which being worn by time, about 1644, Sir Laurence of Chelsea (no kin to him) at his own proper cost and charges, erected to his memory a handsome fair inscription of marble.

His head was upon London Bridge: there goes this story in the family, viz. that one day as one of his daughters was passing under the bridge, looking on her father's head, said she 'That head has lain many a time in my lap, would to God it would fall into my lap as I pass under.' She had her wish, and it did fall into her lap and is now preserved in a vault in the cathedral church at Canterbury. The descendant of Sir Thomas, is Mr More, of Chilston in Herefordshire, where, among a great many things of value plundered by the soldiers, was his jaw, which they kept for a relic. Methinks 'tis strange that all this time he is not canonised; for he merited highly of the church.

Memorandum – in the hall of Sir John Lenthall, at Bessils-Lye in Berkshire, is an original of Sir Thomas and his father, mother, wife and children, done by Hans Holbein. There is an inscription in golden letters of about sixty lines, which I spoke to Mr Thomas Pigot of Wadham College to transcribe, and he has done it very carefully. Ask him for it.

KATHERINE PHILIPS
1631–64

Orinda – From Mr J. Oxenbridge, her uncle (now prisoner in the Fleet on her account for a debt of her husband, that is, that bound for him twenty-eight years since), and Lady Montagu.

Mrs Katherine Fowler was the daughter of John Fowler of London, merchant (an eminent merchant in Bucklesbury), and Katherine Oxenbridge, daughter of Dr Oxenbridge, MD, President of the Physicians' College – look this up in the London Dispensatory.

She was christened in Woolchurch. If alive now (July 1681), she might be forty-eight or forty-nine; see register.

Katherine, the daughter of John Fowler and Katherine his wife, was baptised 11th January, 1631, as per the register book of St Mary's Woolchurch appears.

She went to school at Hackney to Mrs Salmon, a famous schoolmistress, Presbyterian, who used John Ball's catechism. Friends: Mrs Mary Aubrey and Mrs Harvey since, Lady Deering. Loved poetry at school, and made verses there. She takes after her grandmother Oxenbridge, her grandmother, who was an acquaintance of Mr Francis Quarles, being much inclined to poetry herself.

Married to James Philips of the Priory at Cardigan, esq., about 1647 (that is the year after the army was at Putney), by whom she had one son, dead (in her book), and one daughter married to Mr Wgan, in some degree like her mother.

She was very religiously devoted when she was young; prayed by herself an hour together, and took sermons verbatim when she was but ten years old.

She died of the smallpox in Fleet Street. She lies buried at St Benet Sherehog at the end of Syth's Lane in London.

She was when a child much against the bishops, and prayed to God to take them to him, but afterwards was reconciled to them. Prayed aloud, as the hypocritical fashion then was, and was overheard – see Thomas Hobbes's *Civil Wars* and *Satire against Hypocrites*.

My cousin Montague told me that she had a red pimpled face; wrote out verses in inns, or mottos in windows, in her table book.

Memorandum – *La Solitude* de St Amant was englished by Mrs Katherine Philips. 'Tis twenty stanzas – I think not yet printed – I had them from Elizabeth, the Countess of Thanet, 1672.

She went into Ireland (after her marriage) with the Lady Dungannon (whom she calls *Lucatia*); and at Dublin she wrote *Pompey*.

Her husband had a good estate, but bought Crown lands; he mortgaged, etc. His brother Hector took off the mortgages and has the lands.

From her cousin Blacket, who lived with her from her swaddling clothes to eight, and taught her to read. She informs me viz. – when a child she was mighty apt to learn, and she assures me that she had read the Bible through before she was a full four years old; she could have said I know not how many places of scripture and chapters. She was a frequent hearer of sermons; had an excellent memory and could have brought away a sermon in her memory. Very good-natured, not at all high-minded; pretty fat, not tall, reddish faced.

Major General Skippon was her mother's third husband.

She lies interred under a gravestone with her father and grandfather and grandmother, just opposite to the door of the opposite wall; and ask if any inscription on her relations on the said stone.

THOMAS RANDOLPH
1605–35

Thomas Randolph, the poet, Cambridge – I have sent to Anthony Wood his nativity, etc., which I had from his brother John, an attorney. Thomas Randolph was the eldest son of William Randolph by his wife Elizabeth Smyth; he was born at Newnham near Daventry in Northamptonshire, 15th June 1605.

At the age of nine years, he wrote the history of our Saviour's incarnation in English verse, which his brother John has to show under his own handwriting – never printed, kept as rarity.

From Mr Needler – his hair was of a very light flaxen, almost white (like J. Scroope's). It was flaggy,[57] as by his picture before his books appears. He was of a pale ill complexion and pock-pitten – from Mr Thomas Fludd, his schoolfellow at Westminster, who says he was of about my stature or scarce so tall.

His father was steward to Sir George Goring in Sussex. He had been very wild in his youth; and his father (i.e. grandfather to Thomas Randolph) left him but a groat or 3d in his will, which when he received he nailed to the post of the door. His father was a surveyor of land, i.e. a land measurer.

In 1623 he was elected to Trinity College in Cambridge.

In ... he re-encountered Captain Stafford (an ingenious gentleman, and the chief of his family, and out of which the great Duke of Buckinghamshire branched) on the road. He gave him a pension of I think one hundred pounds per annum, and he was tutor to his son and heir.

He was very precocious, and had he lived but a little longer would have outlived his fame.

He died in the twenty-eighth year of his age at Mr William Stafford's, Blatherwycke, aforesaid; was there buried 17th March, 1634, in the aisle of that church among that noble family.

Sir Christopher, Lord Hatton, erected to his memory a monument of white marble – as his epitaph; I think Anthony Wood has it.

SIR HENRY SAVILE
1549–1622

Sir Henry Savile, knight, was born in Yorkshire. He was a younger (or son of a younger) brother, not born to a foot of land. He came to Merton College Oxford (1565); made warden there (1585).

He was a learned gentleman, as most was of the time. He would fain have been thought (I have heard Mr Hobbes say) to have been as great a scholar as Joseph Scaliger. But as for mathematics, I have heard Dr Wallis say that he looked on him to be as able a mathematician as any of his time. He was an extraordinarily handsome and beautiful man; no lady had a finer complexion.

Queen Elizabeth favoured him much; he read (I think) Greek and politics to her. He was also preferred to be Provost of Eton College (1596).

He was a very severe governor, the scholars hated him for his austerity. He could not abide *wits*: when a young scholar was recommended to him for a good wit, 'Out upon him, I'll have nothing to do with him; give me the plodding student. If I would look for wits I would go to Newgate, there be the wits;' and John Earles (afterwards Bishop of Salisbury) was the only scholar that he ever took as recommended for a wit, which was from Dr William Goodwyn, Dean of Christ Church.

He was not only a severe governor, but old Mr Yates (who was fellow in his time) would make lamentable complaints of him to his dying day, that he did oppress the fellows grievously, and he was so great and a favourite to the queen, that there was no dealing with him; his fault was that he was too much inflated with his learning and riches.

He was very munificent, as appears by the two lectures he has given of astronomy and geometry. Bishop Seth Ward, of Salisbury, has told me that he first sent for Mr Edmund Gunter, from London, (being of Oxford University) to have been his professor of geometry: so he came and brought with him his sector and quadrant, and fell to resolving of triangles and doing a great many fine things. Said the grave knight, 'Do you call this reading of geometry? This is showing of tricks, man!' and so dismissed him with scorn, and sent for Henry Briggs, from Cambridge.

I have heard Dr Wallis say that Sir H. Savile has sufficiently confuted Joseph Scaliger *de Quadrata Circuli*,[58] in the very margin of the book: and that sometimes when J. Scaliger says 'AB=CD *ex constructione*',[59] Sir H. Savile writes sometimes in the margin, '*Et dominatio vestra est asinus ex constructione*.'[60]

He left only one daughter, which was married to Sir Charles Sedley of Kent, mother to this present Sir Charles Sedley, who well resembles his grandfather Savile in the face, but is not so proper a man.

Sir H. Savile died at, and was buried at Eton College, in the chapel, on the south-east side of the chancel, under a fair black marble grave stone.

He had travelled very well, and had a general acquaintance with the learned men abroad; by which means he obtained from beyond sea, out of their libraries, several rare Greek MSS, which he had copied by an excellent amanuensis for the Greek character.

Someone put a trick on him, for he got a friend to send him weekly over to Flanders (I think), the sheets of the curious Chrysostom[61] that were printed at Eton, and translated them into Latin, and printed them in Greek and Latin together, which quite spoiled the sale of Sir Henry's.

Memorandum – he gave his collection of mathematical books to a peculiar little library belonging to the Savilian Professors.

WILLIAM SHAKESPEARE
1564–1616

Mr William Shakespeare was born at Stratford upon Avon in the county of Warwickshire. His father was a butcher, and I have been told heretofore by some of the neighbours, that when he was a boy he exercised his father's trade, but when he killed a calf he would do it in a high style, and make a speech. There was at that time another butcher's son in this town that was held not at all inferior to him for a natural wit, his acquaintance and contemporary, but died young.

This William being inclined naturally to poetry and acting, came to London, I guess about eighteen, and was an actor at one of the playhouses, and did act exceedingly well (now B. Jonson was never a good actor, but an excellent instructor).

He began early to make essays at dramatic poetry, which at that time was very low; and his plays took well.

He was a handsome, well shaped man: very good company, and of a very ready and pleasant smooth wit.

The humour of the constable in *A Midsummer Night's Dream*,[62] he happened to take at Grendon in Buckingham-shire – I think it was Midsummer night that he happened to lie there – which is the road from London to Stratford, and there was living that constable about 1642, when I first came to Oxford: Mr Josias Howe is of that parish, and knew him. Ben Jonson and he did gather humours of men daily wherever they came. One time as he was at the tavern at Stratford upon Avon, one Combes, an old rich usurer, was to be buried, he makes there this exemplary epitaph,

Ten in the hundred the Devil allows,
But Combes will have twelve, he swears and vows:
If any one asks who lies in this tomb,
'Hoh!' quoth the Devil, ''Tis my John o Combe.'

He was wont to go to his native country once a year. I think I have been told that he left two or three hundred pounds per annum there or thereabout to a sister. See his epitaph in Dugdale's Warwickshire.

I have heard Sir William Davenant and Mr Thomas Shadwell (who is counted the best comedian we have now) say that he had a most prodigious wit, and did admire his natural parts beyond all other dramatical writers. He was wont to say

(B. Jonson's *Underwoods*) that he 'never blotted out a line in his life'; said Ben Jonson, 'I wish he had blotted out a thousand.'

His comedies will remain wit as long as the English tongue is understood, for that he handles *mores hominum*.[63] Now our present writers reflect so much on particular persons and coxcombities, that twenty years hence they will not be understood.

Though, as Ben Jonson says of him, that he had but a little Latin and less Greek, he understood Latin pretty well, for he had been in his younger years a schoolmaster in the country – from Mr Beeston.

SIR PHILIP SIDNEY
1554–86

Sir Philip Sidney, knight, was the most accomplished cavalier of his time. He was the eldest son of the right honourable Sir Henry Sidney, knight of the noble order of the Garter, Lord President of Wales and Lord Deputy of Ireland, 1570. I suppose he was born at Penhurst in Kent (near Tunbridge).

He had the best tutors provided for him by his father that could be had.

He travelled France, Italy, Germany; he was in the Poland wars, and at that time he had to his page (and as an excellent accomplishment) Henry Danvers (afterwards Earl of Danby), then second son of John Danvers of Dauntsey in Wiltshire, who accounted himself happy that his son was so bestowed. He makes mention, in his *Art of Poesie*, of his being in Hungary (I remember).

He was not only of an excellent wit, but extremely beautiful; he much resembled his sister, but his hair was not red, but a little inclining, viz. a dark amber colour. If I were to find a fault in it, methinks 'tis not masculine enough; yet he was a person of great courage. He was much at Wilton with his sister, and at Ivychurch (which adjoins to the park pale of Clarendon Park), situated on a hill that overlooks all the country westwards, and north over Salisbury and the plains, and into that delicious park (which was accounted the best of England) eastwards. It was heretofore a monastery (the cloisters remain still); 'twas called the monastery of Edros. My great uncle, Mr Thomas Browne, remembered him, and said that he was often wont, as he was hunting on our pleasant plains, to take his table book out of his pocket, and write down his notions as they came into his head, when he was writing his *Arcadia* (which was never finished by him).

He was the reviver of poetry in those dark times, which was then at a very low ebb – e.g. *The Pleasant Comedy of Jacob and Esau*, acted before King Henry VIII's grace (where, I remember, is this expression, that 'the pottage was so good, that God Almighty might have put his finger in't'); *Grammar Gurton's Needle*; and in these plays there is not three lines but there is 'by God', or 'by God's wounds'.

He was of a very munificent spirit, and liberal to all lovers of learning, and to those that pretended to any acquaintance with Parnassus; in so much that he was cloyed and surfeited with the poetasters of those days. Among others Mr Edmund Spenser made his address to him, and bought his *Faerie Queene*. Sir Philip was busy at his study, and his servant delivered Mr Spenser's book to his master, who laid it by, thinking it might be such a kind of stuff as he was frequently troubled with. Mr Spenser stayed so long that his patience was wearied, and went his way discontented, and never intended to come again. When Sir Philip perused it, he was so exceedingly delighted with it, that he was extremely sorry he was gone, and where to send for him he knew not. After much enquiry he learned his lodging, and sent for him, mightily caressed him, and ordered his servant to give him — pounds in gold. His servant said that was too much; 'No,' said Sir Philip, 'he is extraordinary,' and ordered an addition. From this time there was a great friendship between them, to his dying day.

I have heard Dr Pell say, that he has been told by ancient gentlemen of those days of Sir Philip, so famous for men at arms, that 'twas then held as great a disgrace for a young gentleman to be seen riding in the street in a coach as it would now for such a one to be seen in the streets in a petticoat and waistcoat; so much is the fashion of the times now altered.

He married the daughter of Sir Francis Walsingham, Principal Secretary of Estate (I think his only child – ask), whom he loved very well.

Having received some shot or wound in the wars in the Low Countries, where he had command of (the Ramikins, I think), he acted contrary to the injunction of his physicians and surgeons, which cost him his life: upon which occasion there were some roguish verses made.

His body was put in a leaden coffin (which, after the firing of St Paul's, I myself saw), and with wonderful great state was carried to St Paul's Church, where he was buried in Our Lady's chapel: see Sir William Dugdale's *Paul's*, and epitaph. There solemnised this funeral all the nobility and great officers of court; all the judges and sergeants at law; all the soldiers, and commanders, and gentry that were in London; the Lord Mayor, and aldermen, and livery men. His body was borne on men's shoulders (perhaps 'twas a false coffin).

When I was a boy nine years old, I was with my father at one Mr Singleton's, an alderman and woollen-draper in

Gloucester, who had in his parlour, over the chimney, the whole description of the funeral, engraved and printed on papers pasted together, which, at length, was, I believe, the length of the rooms at least; but he had contrived it to be turned upon two pins, that turning one of them made the figures march all in order. It did make such a strong impression on my young fantasy, that I remember it as if it were yesterday. I could never see it elsewhere. The house is in the great long street, over against the high steeple; and 'tis likely it remains there still. 'Tis pity it is not redone.

In St Mary's Church at Warwick is a sumptuous monument of the Lord Brooke, round a great altar of black marble is only this inscription:

England, Netherlands, the Heavens and the Arts
Of ... Sydney hath made ... parts;
... for who could suppose,
That one heap of stones could Sydney enclose.

Key of Pembroke's Arcadia[64]

Sir,
All the good bodies thank you for your remembrance, which I ought to have told you sooner if a pain in my head had not hindered me.

I wish I could give you the key you desire, but all I know of it is not worth anything; though conversant among his relations, could learn no more than Pamela's being my Lady Northumberland, Philoclea my Lady Rich, two sisters, the last beloved by him, upon whose account he made his *Astrophel and Stella*; Miso, Lady Cox, Mopse, Lady Lucy, persons altogether unknown now; Musidorus and Pericles, the two ladies' husbands. Lord Rich being then his friend, he persuaded her mother to the match, though he repented afterwards: she then very young and secretly in love with him but he no concern for her. Her beauty augmenting, he says in his *Astrophel and Stella*, he didn't think 'the morn would have proved so fair a day.' Their mother was beautiful and gallant (whether he meant Ginesia by her or no, I know not); but their father died, they being young. She remarried to Dudley (Leicester and Northumberland), and afterwards to her gentleman of the horse, Sir Christopher Blunt, which was beheaded with Lord Essex. It was thought he meant himself by Amphialus and his lady, Sir Francis Walsingham's daughter and heir, the Queen of Corinth. If he did make his own character high, they said Philisides was himself to, but it was all a guess. He made it young, and dying desired his follies might be burnt.

Some other I have heard guessed at, but have forgotten. Therefore cannot satisfy the lady, which I would for your sake.

I give you thanks but shall not want my grandmother's epitaph (which was for a relation of ours here, who desired it), having found it of your giving.

I knew nothing of my brother's place, but know nothing of his marrying yet.

My service to your brother. I am sorry all things should not answer both your desires.

You have perfectly the good wishes of,

Your humble servant,
D. Tyndale

EDMUND SPENSER
1553-99

Mr Edmund Spenser was of Pembroke Hall in Cambridge; he missed the fellowship there which Bishop Andrews got. He was an acquaintance and frequenter of Sir Erasmus Dryden. His mistress, Rosalind, was a kinswoman of Sir Erasmus' lady's. The chamber there at Sir Erasmus' is still called Mr Spenser's chamber. Lately, at the college taking down the wainscot of his chamber, they found an abundance of cards, with stanzas of the *Faerie Queene* written on them. – From John Dryden, esq., Poet Laureate.

Mr Beeston says he was a little man, wore short hair, little band and little cuffs.

Mr Samuel Woodford (the poet, who paraphrased the Psalms) lives in Hampshire near Alton, and he told me that Mr Spenser lived sometime in these parts, in this delicate sweet air; where he enjoyed his muse, a wrote good part of his verses. I have said before that Sir Phillip Sydney and Sir Walter Raleigh were his acquaintances. He had lived sometime in Ireland, and wrote a description of it, which is printed with Morison's *History, or Description of Ireland*.

Sir John Denham told me, that Archbishop Usher, Lord Primate of Armagh, was acquainted with him, by this token: when Sir William Davenant's *Gondibert* came forth, Sir John asked the Lord Primate if he had seen it. Said the Primate, 'Out upon him, with his vaunting preface, he speaks against my old friend, Edmund Spenser.'

In the south cross-aisle of Westminster Abbey, next the door, is this inscription:

Heare lies (expecting the second coming of our Saviour Christ Jesus) the body of Edmund Spenser, the Prince of Poets of his tyme; whose divine spirit needs no other witness than the works which he left behind him. He was born in London, in the yeare 1510 and dyed in the yeare 1596.

SIR JOHN SUCKLING
1609-42

Sir John Suckling, knight, was the eldest son of Sir John Suckling, of the Green Cloth[65] in the time of, I think, Charles I. He was born February 1609.

I have heard Mrs Bond say, that Sir John's father was but a dull fellow (her husband, Mr Thomas Bond, knew him): the wit came by the mother.

Ask Dr Busby if he was not of Westminster School? He might be about his time. I have heard Sir William Davenant say he went to the University of Cambridge at eleven years of age, where he studied three or four years (I think four). By eighteen he had well travelled France and Italy, and part of Germany, and (I think also) of Spain.

He returned into England an extraordinarily accomplished gentleman, grew famous at court for his ready sparkling wit which was envied, and he was (Sir William said) the bull that was baited. He was incomparably ready at reparteeing, and his wit was most sparkling when most set upon and provoked.

He was the greatest gallant of his time, and the greatest gamester, both for bowling and cards, so that no shopkeeper would trust him for 6d, as today, for instance, he might, by winning, be worth two hundred pounds, the next day he might not be worth half so much, or perhaps be sometime less than nothing. Sir William (who was his intimate friend, and loved him entirely) would say that Sir John, when he was at his lowest ebb in gaming, I mean then unfortunate, then would make himself most glorious in apparel, and said that it exalted his spirits, and that he had then best luck when he was most gallant, and his spirits were highest.

Sir William would say that he did not much care for a lord's converse, for they were in those days damnably proud and arrogant and the French would say that 'My Lord d'Angleterre ... comme un mastiff-dog;' but now the age is more refined, and much by the example of His Gracious Majesty, who is the pattern of courtesy.

In 163- there happened, unluckily, a difference between Sir John Suckling and Sir John Digby (brother to Sir Kenelm) about a mistress or gaming, I have now forgotten. Sir John was but a slight-timbered man, and of middling stature; Sir John Digby a proper person of great strength, and courage answerable, and yielded to be the best swordsman of his time. Sir John, with some two or three of his party assaults Sir John Digby going into a playhouse; Sir J.D. had only his lackey with him, but he flew on them like a tiger, and made them run. 'Twas pity that this accident brought the blemish of cowardice to such an ingenious young spark. Sir J.D. was such a hero that there were very few but he would have served in the like manner.

In 163-, when the expedition was gone into Scotland, Sir John Suckling, at his own charge, raised a troop of a hundred very handsome young proper men, whom he clad in white doublets and scarlet breeches, and scarlet coats, hats and feathers, well horsed, and armed. They say 'twas one of the finest sights in those days. But Sir John Menis made a lampoon of it (see the old collection of lampoons):

The ladies opened the windows to see
So fine and goodly a sight-a, etc.

I think the lampoon says he made an inglorious charge against the Scots.

Ask in what army he was in the civil wars.

He went into France, where after some time being come to the bottom of his fund that was left, reflecting on the miserable and despicable condition he should be reduced to, having nothing left to maintain him, he (having a convenience for that purpose, lying at an apothecary's house, in Paris) took poison, which killed him miserably with vomiting. He was buried in the Protestants' churchyard. This was (to the best of my remembrance) 1646.

His picture, which is like him, before his *Poems*, says that he was but twenty-eight when he died.

He was of middle stature and slight strength, brisk round eye, reddish faced and red nose (ill liver), his head not very big, his hair a kind of sand colour; his beard turned up naturally, so that he had a brisk and graceful look. He died a bachelor.

Memorandum – he made a magnificent entertainment in London, for a great number of ladies of quality, all beauties and young, which cost him hundreds of pounds, where were all the rarities that this part of the world could afford, and the last service of all was silk stockings and garters, and I think also gloves.

In 1637 Sir John Suckling, William Davenant, Poet Laureate (not then knighted) and Jack Young came to the Bath. Sir John came like a young prince for all the manner of equipage and convenience, and Sir W. Davenant told me that he had a cart-load of books carried down, and 'twas there, at Bath, that he wrote the little tract in his book about Socinianism.[66] 'Twas as pleasant a journey as ever men had; in the height of a long peace and luxury, and in the venison season. The second night they lay at Marlborough, and walking on the delicate fine downs at the backside of the town, whilst supper was making ready, the maids were drying of clothes on the bushes. Jack Young had espied a very pretty young girl, and had got her consent for an assignation, which was about midnight, which they happened to overhear on the other side of the hedge, and were resolved to frustrate his design. They were wont every night to play at cards after supper a good while; but Jack Young pretended weariness, etc. and must needs go to bed, not to be persuaded by any means to the contrary. They had their landlady at supper with them; said they to her, 'Observe this poor gentleman how he yawns, now is his mad fit coming upon him. We beseech you that you make fast his doors, and get somebody to watch and look to him, for about midnight he will fall to be most outrageous: get the ostler, or some strong fellow, to stay up, and we will well content him, for he is our worthy friend, and a very honest gentleman, only, perhaps, twice a year he falls into these fits.' Jack Young slept not, but was ready to go out as the clock struck to the hour of his appointment, and then going to open the door he was disappointed, knocks, bounces, calls 'Tapster! Chamberlayne! Ostler!' swears and curses dreadfully; nobody would come to him. Sir John and W. Davenant were expectant all this time, and ready to die with laughter. I know not how he happened to get open the door, and was coming downstairs. The ostler, a huge, lusty fellow, fell upon him, and held him, and cried. 'Good sir, take God in your mind, you shall not go out to destroy yourself.' J. Young struggled and strived, insomuch that at last he was quite spent and dispirited, and fain to go to bed to rest himself. In the morning the landlady of the house came to see how he did, and brought him a caudle. 'Oh sir,' said she, 'you had a heavy fit last night, pray, sir, be pleased to take some of this to comfort your heart.' Jack Young thought the woman had been mad, and being exceedingly vexed, flirted the porringer of caudle in her face. The next day his comrades told him all the plot, how they cross-bit him. That night they went to Bronham House, Sir Edward Baynton's (then a noble seat, since burnt in the civil wars) where they were nobly entertained several days. From thence, they went to West Kington, to Parson Davenant, Sir William's eldest brother, where they stayed a week – mirth, wit and good cheer flowing. From thence to Bath, six or seven miles.

Memorandum – Parson Robert Davenant has told me that that tract about Socinianism was written on the table in the parlour of the parsonage at West Kington.

My Lady Southcot, whose husband hanged himself, was Sir John Suckling's sister, to whom he writes a consolatory letter, viz. the first. She afterwards married Dr Corbet, DD, of Merton College Oxford. At her house in Bishopsgate Street, London, is an original of her brother, Sir John, of Sir Anthony Van Dyke, all at length, leaning against a rock, with a playbook, contemplating. It is a piece of great value. There is also another rare picture, viz. of that pretty creature, Mrs Jane Shore, an original.

When his *Aglaura* was acted, he bought all the clothes himself, which were very rich; no tinsel, all the lace pure gold and silver, which cost him … I have now forgotten. He had some scenes to it, which in those days were only used at masques.

Memorandum – Mr Snowdon tells me, that after Sir John's unlucky encounter, or quarrel, with Sir John Digby, wherein he was baffled: 'twas strange to see the envy and ill nature of people to trample and scoff at, and deject one in disgrace; inhumane as well as unchristian. The Lady Moray (query) had made an entertainment for several persons of quality at Ashley (in Surrey, near Chertsey), whereat Mr Snowdon then was. There was the Countess of Middlesex, whom Sir John had highly courted, and had spent on her, and in treating her, some thousands of pounds. At this entertainment she could not forbear, but was so severe and ingrate as to upbraid Sir John of his late received baffle; and some other ladies had their flirts. The Lady Moray (who invited them) seeing Sir John out of countenance, for whose worth she always had respect: 'Well,' said she, 'I am a merry wench, and will never forsake an old friend in disgrace, so come sit down by me, Sir John' (said she), and seated him on her right hand, and countenanced him. This raised Sir John's dejected spirits that he threw his repartees about the table with so much sparklingness and gentleness of wit, to the admiration of them all.

Sir John Suckling – from Mr William Beeston – invented the game of cribbage. He sent his cards to all gaming places in the country, which were marked with private marks of his: he got twenty thousand pounds this way. Sir Francis Cornwallis made *Aglaura*, except the end.

HENRY VAUGHAN
1621–95
THOMAS VAUGHAN
1621–67

There are two Vaughans, twins, both very ingenious and writers. One wrote a poem called *Olor Iscanus* (Henry Vaughan, the firstborn), and another book of divine meditations. His brother wrote several treatises, whose names I have now forgotten, but names himself *Eugenius Philalethes*.

They were born at Llansanfraid in Brecknockshire, by the river Usk (Isca). Their grandmother was an Aubrey: their father, a coxcomb, and no honester than he should be – he cozened me of 50s. once.

Eugenius Philalethes was of Jesus College. Whither Henry was I have forgotten; but he was a clerk sometime to Judge Sir Marmaduke Lloyd.

Henry Vaughan, 'Silurist' – you know Silures[67] contained Brecknockshire, Herefordshire, etc.

A letter from Henry Vaughan to Aubrey

My brother and I were born at Newton, in Brecknockshire, in the parish of St Bridget's, in the year 1621.

I stayed not at Oxford to take my degree, but was sent to London, being then designed by my father for the study of the law, which the sudden eruption of our late civil wars wholly frustrated.

My brother continued there for ten or twelve years, and I think he could be no less than Master of Arts. He died upon an employment for His Majesty, within five or six miles of Oxford, in the year that this last great plague visited London. He was buried by Sir Robert Moray, his great friend (and then secretary of estate for the kingdom of Scotland); to whom he gave his books and MSS.

My profession is also physic, which I have practised now for many years with good success (I thank God) and a repute big enough for a person of greater parts than myself.

EDWARD DE VERE
SEVENTEENTH EARL OF OXFORD
1550–1604

Mr Thomas Henshaw, Fellow of the Royal Society, tells me that Nicholas Hill was secretary to Edward de Vere, the great Earl of Oxford, who spent forty thousand pounds per annum in seven years' travel. He lived in Florence in more grandeur than the Duke of Tuscany.

This Earl of Oxford, making of his low obeisance to Queen Elizabeth, happened to fart, at which he was so abashed that he went to travel seven years. On his return the queen welcomed him home and said, 'My Lord, I had forgotten the fart.'

A poor man asked of Mr Hill one time to give him 6d (or 1s or such as alms). Said Mr Hill 'What do you say, if I give you ten pounds?' 'Oh!' said he, 'ten pounds would make me a man.' And he did put it down in the account – 'Item, ten pounds, for making a man' – which his lordship allowed and was pleased at it.

EDMUND WALLER
1606–87

Edmund Waller, esq., son and heir of Robert Waller by Anne Hamden. He was cousin-german to Oliver Cromwell, Protector, whose mother was his mother's sister.

He was born at Beaconsfield in Buckinghamshire, in the fair brick house, the farthest on the left hand, as you go to Wycombe.

He had grammar learning from the information of Mr Gerard Dobson, minister of High Wycombe, who taught a private school there, and was (he told me) a good school-master, and had been bred at Eton College school. I have heard Mr Thomas Bigge, of Wycombe, say (who was his schoolfellow, and of the same form), that he little thought then he would have been so rare a poet; he was wont to make his exercise for him.

His paternal estate, and by his first wife, was three thousand pounds per annum. His second wife was Mary Bracey; a woman beautiful and very prudent, by whom he has several children (I think ten or twelve).

About twenty-three, or between that and thirty, he grew (upon I know not what occasion) mad; but 'twas (I think) not long ere he was cured – this from Mr Thomas Bigge.

Non tulit aethereos pectus mortale tumultus.[68]
Ovid

Memorandum – he was proud: to such, a check often gives that distemper.

He was passionately in love with Dorothea, the eldest daughter of the Earl of Leicester, whom he has eternised in his poems: and the earl loved him, and would have been contented that he should have had one of the youngest daughters: perhaps *this* might be the check.

Waller (I think Walter) was his tutor at King's College, Cambridge, who was a very learned man, and afterwards vicar of Broad Chalk, Wiltshire.

A Member of Parliament for Beaconsfield in King James's time, and has been of all the Parliaments since the restoration of King Charles II.

One of the first refiners of our English language and poetry. When he was a brisk young spark, and first studied poetry,

'Methought,' said he, 'I never saw a good copy of English verses; they want smoothness; then I began to essay.' I have several times heard him say, that he cannot versify when he will, but when the fit comes upon him, he does it easily, i.e. in plain terms, when his Mercurius and Venus are well aspected.

He told me he was not acquainted with Ben Jonson (who died about 1638), but familiarly with Lucius, Lord Falkland, Sydney Godophin, Mr Hobbes, etc.

He was very much admired at court before the late civil wars. 164-, he being then a member of the Houses of Commons, he was committed prisoner to the Tower, for the plot, with Nathaniel Tomkins (his cousin-german) and Richard Chaloner, for firing the City of London, and delivering the Parliament, etc. to the king's party. He had much ado then to save his life, and in order to it, sold his estate in Bedfordshire, about one thousand three hundred pounds per annum, to Dr Wright, MD, for ten thousand pounds (much under value) which was procured in twenty-four hours' time, or else he had been hanged (ask E. Wyld, esq.). With which money he bribed the whole House, which was the first time a House of Commons was ever bribed. His excellent rhetorical speech to the House (see his speech to save his life), as also his panegyric to Oliver, Lord Protector, he would not suffer to be inserted in the edition of his poems since the restoration of King Charles II.

After he had obtained his pardon of the Parliament, he went to France, where he stayed … years, and was there very kindly received, and esteemed.

When King Charles II returned, he received Mr Waller very kindly, and no man's conversation is more esteemed at court now than his. The Duchess of York (daughter to the Duke of Modena) very much delights in his company, and has laid her commands on him to write, which he has dedicated to her highness.

His intellectuals are very good yet (1680), and makes verses; but he grows feeble. He wrote verses of the Bermudas fifty years since, upon the information of one that had been there; walking in his fine woods, the poetic spirit came upon him.

He is of somewhat above a middle stature, thin body, not at all robust: fine thin skin, his face somewhat of an olive complexion; his hair frizzed, of a brownish colour; full eye, popping out and working; oval faced, his forehead high and full of wrinkles. His head but small, brain very hot, and apt to be choleric – *Quanto doctor, eo iracundior* [69] – Cicero. He is something magisterial, and has a great mastership of the English language. He is of admirable and graceful elocution, and exceeding ready.

He has spent most of his time in London, especially in winter; but oftentimes in the summer he enjoys his muse at Beaconsfield, which is incomparable air, and where are delicious walks in the woods. Now I speak of woods, I remember he told us there, that he cut down and grubbed up a beech wood of his, at Beaconsfield in Buckinghamshire, and without sowing, but naturally, there grew up a wood all of birch.

He was admitted a Fellow of the Royal Society.

He has but a tender weak body, but was always very temperate. Someone (ask Samuel Butler) made him damnable drunk at Somerset House, where, at the water stairs, he fell down, and had a cruel fall. 'Twas pity to use such a sweet swan so inhumanely.

He has a great memory, and remembers a history, etc. best when read to him: he used to make his daughters read to him. Yet, notwithstanding his great wit and mastership in rhetoric, etc. he will oftentimes be guilty of misspelling in English. He writes a lamentably bad hand, as bad as the scratching of a hen.

I have heard him say that he so much admired Mr Thomas Hobbes' book *De Cive*, when it came forth, that he was very desirous to have it done into English, and Mr Hobbes was most willing it should be done by Mr Waller's hand, for that he was so great a master of our English language. Mr Waller freely promised him to do it, but first he would desire Mr Hobbes to make an essay; he (T.H.) did the first book, and did it so extremely well, that Mr Waller would not meddle with it, for nobody else could do it so well. Had he thought he could have better performed it, he would have himself been the translator.

Memorandum – his speech against ship money which is in his book of poems: his panegyric to Oliver the Protector I have: and also to King Charles II.

He says that he was bred under several ill, dull, ignorant schoolmasters, till he went to Mr Dobson, at Wycombe, who was a good schoolmaster, and had been an Eton scholar.

Memorandum – later end of August 1680, he wrote verses called *Divine Love* at the instance and request of the lady Viscountess Ranulagh.

He missed the Provostship of Eton College (February 1680). Zachary Craddock has it.

He lies buried in the churchyard (south-east of the church), where his grandfather and father were buried. This burying place is railed about like a pound, and about that bigness. There is a walnut tree planted, that is, perhaps, fifty years old: (the walnut tree is their crest). There are nine graves or *cippi*;[70] no gravestone or inscription.

From Captain Edmund Hamden, his cousin-german, 1690 – Edmund Waller esq. was born in the parish of Amersham, in Buckinghamshire, at a place called Winchmore Hill, which was sold by his father, and which he had a very great desire to have bought again, not long before his death, but the owner would not sell it: part of the house has been new-built, but the room wherein he was born is yet standing. Said he, to his cousin Hamden, 'A stag, when he is hunted, and near spent, always returns home.' He died at eighty-three, and his wit was as florid then as at any time of his life. He derived his poetic wit from the Hamdens; several of them have been poets.

Whereas Rutt, that kept the Inn (the Crown, I think) at Beaconsfield, told me, many years since, that he had been distempered; Captain Hamden affirms it is false; but his brother was a fool, as to discourse or business, but was very learned. And whereas Dr Peter Birch told me that he had a prodigious memory; his sons affirm that he had no good memory, and was never good to learn a thing by heart, but some things that pleased him he did strongly retain.

Captain Hamden told me that the soldiers came to Beaconsfield to search for money; his mother told them if they would go along with her, she would show them where she had buried five thousand pounds, and had them to the house of office.

Mr Christopher Wase repeating to him the bitter satirical verses made on Sir Carre Scroop, viz. –

The brother murdered, and thy sister whored,
Thy mother too – and yet thy pen's thy sword;

Mr Waller replied *sur le champ*[71] 'that men write ill things well and good things ill; that satirical writing was downhill, most easy and natural; that at Billingsgate one might hear great heights of such wit; that the cursed earth naturally produces briars and thorns and weeds, but roses and fine flowers require cultivation.'

All his writings are free from offence.

His poems are reprinted now (1682) by his own orders and his pictures (young and old) before it, and underneath:

Sed Carmina major imago.[72]

He made some verses of his own dying, but a fortnight, or little more, before his decease.

JOHN WILMOT
SECOND EARL OF ROCHESTER
1647–80

John, Earl of Rochester – he went to school at Burford; was of Wadham College, Oxford; I suppose, had been in France.

About eighteen, he stole his lady, Elizabeth Malet, a daughter and heir, a great fortune; for which I remember I saw him prisoner in the Tower about 1662.

His youthly spirit and opulent fortune did sometimes make him do extravagant actions, but in the country he was generally civil enough. He was wont to say that when he came to Brentford the Devil entered into him and never left him till he came into the country again to Alderbury or Woodstock.

He was ranger of Woodstock park and lived often at the lodge at the west end, a very delightful place and noble prospect westwards. Here his lordship had several lascivious pictures drawn.

His lordship read all manner of books. Mr Andrew Marvell, who was a good judge of wit, was wont to say that he was the best English satirist and had the right vein. 'Twas pity death took him off so soon.

In his last sickness he was exceedingly penitent and wrote a letter of his repentance to Dr Burnet, which is printed. He sent for all his servants, even the pigherd boy, to come and hear his palinode. He died at Woodstock park 26th July, 1680; and is buried at Spilsbury in the same county, 9th August following.

His immature death puts me in mind of these verses of Propertius:

Vere novo primoque in aetatis flore juventae,
Ceu rosa virgineo police carpta, jaces.[73]

GEORGE WITHERS
1588–1667

Mr George Withers was born at Bentworth, near Alton, in Hampshire, on 11th June, 1588.

He married Elizabeth, eldest daughter of H. Emerson, of South Lambeth, esq., whose ancestors lie entombed in the choir of St Saviour's, Southwark, near the monument of Bishop Andrews, with a statue of white marble. She was a great wit, and would write in verse too.

He was of Magdalen College in Oxford. He would make verses as fast as he could write them. And though he was an easy rhymer, and no good poet, he was a good prophet. He had a strange sagacity and foresight into mundane affairs.

He was an early observer of *Quicquid agunt homines*;[74] his wit was satirical. I think the first thing he wrote was 'Abuses whipped and stripped', for which he was committed prisoner to (I believe) Newgate. I believe 'twas in King James's time. He was a captain in the Parliament army, and the Parliament gave him for his service Mr John Denham's estate at Egham, in Surrey. The motto of his colours was *Pro Rege, Lege, Grege.*[75]

After the restoration of His Majesty he was imprisoned in the Tower about three quarters of a year. He died on the 2nd May, 1667, and lies interred within the east door of the Savoy church, where he died. He was pupil to Bishop John Warner of Rochester.

NOTES

1. Aubrey left gaps in his text, which he intended to return to and complete. In this edition, these are represented by ellipses.

2. George Sandys (1578–1644), English traveller, colonist and poet.

3. This is a reference to Cicero, whose full name was Marcus Tullius Cicero.

4. 'I hate the common crowd and I spurn them' (Latin). Horace, *Odes*, 3, 1, 1.

5. 'What did I do that was worthy, leading this kind of life?' (Latin).

6. 'Itself lacking the ability to cut' (Latin). Horace, *Ars Poetica*, 305.

7. 'The gods above thought otherwise' (Latin).

8. 'In the mount of the Lord it shall be seen' (Latin).

9. 'Gradually' (Latin).

10. Hidden away.

11. Fellow of the Royal Society.

12. 'Like a dog in the Nile' (Latin).

13. 'So I will play the part of a whetstone' (Latin). Horace, *Ars Poetica*, 304.

14. 'Whom I name out of the highest gratitude' (Latin).

15. *On Laws* (Latin).

16. 'And everything of that kind' (Latin).

17. 'Of his own accord and special grace' (Latin).

18. 'The deadly reed fast in the flesh' (Latin). Virgil, *Aeneid*, 73.

19. 'According to justice and honesty' (Latin).

20. Charles I.

21. 'This book is such that no fool could have written it, / nor would a wise man have wished to: that is Hugh's opinion' (Latin).

22. A lead roof on which one could walk.

23. 'There will be another Tiphys' (Latin).

24. 'Failing better things' (Latin).

25. 'We have better counsels' (Latin).

26. Soreness of eyes.

27. A royalist.

28. The deanship.

29. Broke down.

30. i.e. a stallion.

31. Gaius Maecenas (70–8 BC), confidant and advisor to Octavian (who, as Caesar Augustus, became the first Emperor of Rome), and an important patron for the new generation of 'Augustan' poets.

32. 'In the reciting style' (Latin).

33. i.e. scenery.

34. Suppose, while spluttering verses, head on high, / Like fowler watching blackbirds in the sky, / He falls into a pit;' (Latin). Horace, *Ars Poetica*, ll. 457–9, trans. John Conington.

35. i.e. the Jesuits.

36. i.e. on his monument at Westminster Abbey.

37. i.e. they were members of the Waldensian sect, an old dualist heresy.

38. i.e. tutor.

39. A card game popular in the sixteenth and seventeenth centuries.

40. Joseph Scaliger (1540–1609), French religious leader and scholar.

41. Christopher Clavius (1538–1612), German Jesuit mathematician and astronomer.

42. i.e. dawn itself.

43. i.e. Wiltshire.

44. Jean-Louis Guez de Balzac, *Lettres*. Jean-Louis Guez de Balzac (1597–1654), French author.

45. This is a small selection of the acquaintances listed.

46. 'But all of this must remain between us' (Latin).

47. 'But this is irrelevant' (Latin).

48. Member of the governing body of Lincoln's Inn.

49. Aulus Gellius (*c.*125 – *c.*170), Latin author and grammarian.

50. Like an explorer (Latin).

51. Sheriffs were chosen by pricking a list with a bodkin.

52. 'The sparkling eyes; / The hands that Bacchus might not scorn to show, / And hair that round Apollo's head might flow; / With all the purple youthfulness of face, / That gently blushes in the wat'ry glass' (Latin). Ovid, *Metamorphoses* III: Echo and Narcissus. Translated by Sir Samuel Garth, John Dryden, et al.

53. Aubrey's error. Should be third wife.

54. i.e. 1664.

55. A London bookseller.

56. 'Nowhere on his body was there a blemish' (Latin). Ovid, *Amores*, 15, 18.

57. Limp or strawlike.

58. 'On the squaring of the circle' (Latin).

59. 'In construction' (Latin).

60. 'And your rule is an ass by construction' (Latin).

61. Sir John Chrysostom (349–*c.*407), Archbishop of Constantinople.

62. It has been suggested that perhaps Aubrey is referring to Dogberry in *Much Ado About Nothing*.

63. 'The ways of men' (Latin).

64. This is the title given by John Aubrey to a letter by D. Tyndale.

65. Controller of the Royal Household.

66. Socinianism is a form of Antitrinitarianism, a Christian belief system that rejects the doctrine that God is three distinct persons in one being.

67. An ancient British tribe.

68. 'The human heart does not receive its disturbance from the heavens' (Latin).

69. 'The more learned, the more ready to anger' (Latin).

70. 'Tombstones' (Latin).

71. 'Immediately' (French).

72. 'But his songs are a greater image' (Latin). Ovid, *Tristia*, I, vii, 11.

73. 'In the flower of your youth, and in your first new spring, / Like a rose plucked by a young girl's hand, you lie' (Latin).

74. 'Whatever men do' (Latin).

75. 'For king, law and company' (Latin).

INDEX OF SUBJECTS

BIOGRAPHICAL NOTE

Born near Malmesbury in Wiltshire in 1626, John Aubrey was the oldest surviving son of a well-off gentry family. He was educated at Malmesbury Grammar School under Robert Latimer, and it was here he made the acquaintance of Thomas Hobbes, about whom he would later write.

He went on to enter Trinity College, Oxford, but his education was interrupted by the English Civil War. In 1646 he became a student of the Middle Temple.

Aubrey was an antiquary and in 1648, was the first person to discover the ruins of Avebury. He devoted much time to archaeological research and became one of the original fellows of the Royal Society in 1662. Throughout his life, Aubrey was acquainted with the most celebrated writers, scientists and politicians of his day, along with a large number of other distinguished figures,

Miscellanies (1696) was the only work he published during his lifetime. His *Natural History of Wiltshire* was made available in 1847, but he is best remembered for his *Lives of Eminent Men* (sometimes referred to as *Brief Lives*), a series of biographical notes, court gossip and scurrilous anecdotes collected over a number of years.

Aubrey died of apoplexy in June 1697 while travelling, and was buried in the churchyard at St Mary Magdalene, Oxford.

HESPERUS PRESS CLASSICS

Hesperus Press, as suggested by the Latin motto, is committed to bringing near what is far – far both in space and time. Works written by the greatest authors, and unjustly neglected or simply little known in the English-speaking world, are made accessible through new translations and a completely fresh editorial approach. Through these classic works, the reader is introduced to the greatest writers from all times and all cultures.

For more information on Hesperus Press, please visit our website: **www.hesperuspress.com**

ET REMOTISSIMA PROPE